T W I C E B L

ALSO BY JOAN LEONARD

What to Do to Improve Your Child's Manners

Tales from Toddler Hell

TWICE BLESSED

*Everything You Need to
Know About Having a Second
Child—Preparing Yourself, Your
Marriage, and Your Firstborn
for a New Family of Four*

JOAN LEONARD

St. Martin's Griffin   New York

Book design by Kate Nichols

ISBN 0-312-25430-X

D 18 17 16 15 14 13 12

For my sister, Mary Leonard
Blessed to have each other

Contents

Contents

III: A Family of Four

Acknowledgments

This book would never have been written without the help of countless others. I'd like to thank the many mothers and fathers who so generously shared their tales of parenting trials and triumphs. Their stories—both happy and sad—help us all.

The child psychologists, physicians, and other experts I interviewed gave invaluable advice. They were patient with the details and painstaking with their research, especially Elizabeth Ellis, Ph.D., Darcy Pattison, C.S.W., and Millie Willen, M.S.W., who have become my friends as well as advisors.

Pam Abrams at *Child*, Elin McCoy at *Pen and Pencil Books*, and Wendy Schuman at *Parents*, have all helped to strengthen my writing. It is a pleasure to work with them.

Many thanks to Cassie Jones for her sensible and sensitive expertise in editing this book. A big thank you goes to Lara Asher. I couldn't have asked for a more enthusiastic, helpful editor to see the project through.

I owe a debt of gratitude to Lynn Seligman, my agent, who believed in this book all along and encouraged me to write it. It is because of her perseverance and faith in me throughout the years that I have a writing career.

I am indeed lucky to have such supportive parents and good friends; they are wise, witty, and loving. Pals Aphie, Alecia, Cathy, Darcy, John, Katherine, cousin Linda, sister Mary, Monica, Mort, and Roberta have listened to my incessant whining throughout the past year, and miraculously still take my phone calls.

The great Mike McGrady, my mentor as well as my friend, taught me most of what I know about writing, and he continues to guide me through my darker moments of self-doubt.

Finally, it is my own family that I thank most profusely. During the writing siege, my husband, Salvatore, provided me with loving support, well-timed jokes, and fabulous pasta dinners. My son, Alex, got me to take breaks by reading me passages from *Captain Underpants* on rainy afternoons. My daughter, Annie, "tucked me in" at 9:00 P.M. on the nights before I had to get up early the next morning to write.

I am blessed beyond measure.

Introduction

It was not long after our first child, Annie, was born, that I began to plan for our second. My parenting fantasy, after all, had not been centered around having a child so much as having a FAMILY. And to me—growing up as one of two children myself—a family meant a family of four. My husband had been an only child and was just as eager to give Annie a brother or sister.

Still, I admit I had mixed feelings the day I found out I was pregnant again. It had been one of those endless rainy Saturday mornings with no baby-sitter in sight. My husband and I had been taking turns following our very cranky thirteen-month-old around the house as she half crawled, half staggered her way from room to room—taking swipes at anything within reach, pulling down newspapers and junk mail from the countertop, destroying whatever came in her path. I had been feeling out of sorts for weeks—my period was off schedule—and I thought I was coming down with the flu.

By the time the afternoon rolled around, we decided to try the home pregnancy kit—even though it was probably ridiculous to think I'd be pregnant so soon. After all, it had taken almost two years of calculated and well-timed sex for me to get pregnant with Annie. And although we planned on waiting for Annie to have a brother or sister in, say, two or three years, we had been somewhat sloppy in our birth control in the last few months.

At any rate, all three of us ended up in the bathroom. Annie, fixated on her brand new potty, was sitting on it just for fun, her big girl diaper around her ankles. My husband and I were poised like mad scientists over the home pregnancy kit—the glass vial set precariously between the Desinex and the Handi Wipes on the vanity—waiting to see if the clear liquid would turn blue or not.

It turned blue.

"Oh my God," my husband said, plopping down on the toilet seat.

"Oh my God," I said, looking up into the mirror—half expecting to see a werewolf stare back at me.

"Oh my God, oh my God, oh my God," Annie chanted, cheering up considerably at the sight of some high drama in the room.

I did some quick figuring and realized that in nine months I would be following Annie around throughout the house WHILE I was breast-feeding the new baby. And when it was teething at six months, Annie would be right in the middle of the Terrible Twos. Annie, as perfect as she was, required, it seemed, round-the-clock attention from both my husband and me. How would we gather the sheer stamina needed to care for two children? What COULD we have been thinking?

My husband, riveted to the toilet seat, stared off into space.

"We'll need another car seat. A double stroller. Another crib. Another high chair." He glanced over at our daughter, who had succeeded in using her new potty but had, regrettably, aimed poorly. "I'm going to lie down," he said, and disappeared into the bedroom, leaving me to hold the blue vial.

This reaction was, of course, very different from finding out I was pregnant with Annie. That news took on a kind of religious significance; ah, but this time we had an idea of what lay ahead of us. We knew that along with the pure joy a child brings would also be the reality of sleepless nights and exhausting days. This time we thought we knew what to expect.

What we didn't know, however, was how different a second pregnancy could be both physically and emotionally, how the second birth was nothing like the first, how a new baby would affect Annie, and how drastically our lives would change—again!—when we actually became a family of four.

I think it was Nancy on *thirtysomething* who said, "Having two kids is really like having four kids." Only after it happens to you can you understand that line—and heartily agree with it! This book takes a look at all those areas of change as well as the adjustments we all make when a second family member enters our lives. You will hear from dozens of families of four—both moms and dads—who give practical tips from the trenches of parenthood. A variety of gynecologists, pediatricians, and family therapists guide you through both the pleasures and pandemonium of being "twice blessed."

That's what the maternity nurse said to me, by the way, when she laid my son, Alex, in my arms only minutes after he was born. Nineteen months earlier she had helped deliver my daughter.

"Now you're twice blessed," she had whispered, and tiptoed out of the room.

And she was right.

 I

Parenting Your First While Expecting Your Second

1

Preparing Yourself

Deciding to Do It . . . Again

Just when we thought we were finally getting the hang of it.
Our stretch marks have started to fade; we've packed away our
nursing bras and our maternity clothes. Occasionally, we made
time to shave our legs, pluck our eyebrows, moisturize our neck,
paint our toenails. Our face was beginning to lose that deer-
in-headlights look of perpetual panic. Our body—well, although
it never actually went back to its old tight self, at least it was beginning to *go back* a little bit. It even looked as if we might be
having sex with our husbands again on a somewhat regular basis.
Some of us were at the point where we could sail past the diaper
aisle at the local supermarket. Or have a few free hours during
preschool. Or even full-day kindergarten. Others were not only
back at work with solid child care but proceeding nicely on the
fast track to promotion. And sometimes . . . sometimes we actually slept through the night.

Just when things seem to be returning to normal, boom—we decide to do it all over again. Even those of us who had horrendous labors and whose first words after giving birth were, "Well, I'll never go through *that* again!" end up changing our minds.

Why do couples decide to have a second child? One thing is for certain: Never before in history has the two-child family been so popular, and the trend appears to be continuing as we enter the millennium. A century ago, it was common to have four or five children to a family. Back then, birth control didn't exist, and more children meant more help on farms and in family businesses. However, these days, family-planning education, the increase in living costs, and the energy needed to raise a well-adjusted, well-rounded child have led to smaller families. The Bureau of the Census reports that today the average woman is more likely to have two children than any other number. Why is that the case? Factoring in all these considerations, why aren't couples satisfied with only one child? While each case is individual, parents are motivated by several common factors to have a family of four.

"I Want My Child to Have a Sibling"

This appears to be the strongest argument for having two children. Many parents think about their first child when they decide to get pregnant again. It seems it isn't so much that couples want the experience of a second child as much as they want their own child to have a playmate. "I didn't want my son to grow up as an only child like I did," says one mother. "It's just too hard to be the only kid with two adults"; "I'm so close to my own sister that I wanted my daughter to experience that closeness," says another. A father says, "I knew we'd really spoil Kevin rotten unless we had another. We were just too focused on his every whim. It wasn't until we had Kristen that we took our eyes off of him."

"We Wanted One of Each Sex"

Although definitely a gamble—we all know of families with three boys or four girls!—some couples try for one boy and one girl to "make things even." Each wants to identify with his or her own gender. One mom says, "I dreamed of going shopping for clothes and makeup with my daughter when she grew up." Another states, "After our son was born, my husband seemed more involved with child rearing than he had been with just our daughter." On the other hand, talk to mothers of two girls or two boys and often you will find no regrets. Whatever happens seems to work out for the best, and most couples adapt their own expectations to their children's personalities, not their sex.

"One for Me and One for Him"

Some couples feel that two children can even out a family. "Of course we both love both kids, but I'm closer to my son, and my husband is closer to our daughter. It seems like there's one for each of us now," says Barbara. Her husband agrees: "Once my daughter was born, I understood that really strong bond my wife had with Eric. I feel that way about Beth, and it sort of balances everything out."

"A Real Family Means a 'Family of Four'"

Although my friends with one or no children would take umbrage with that definition, to many couples, you need two kids to constitute a family. As my neighbor explains, "With one child, we were a couple with a baby. With two, we're a family!"

Whatever our reasons, however much we all try to control our family and our fate, nature, in the end, takes over. Your second child will be his or her own person, and your experience with him or her will be new and challenging in its own way.

Preparing Yourself

FIRST THOUGHTS ON
FINDING OUT YOU'RE PREGNANT

FIRST TIME:

SECOND TIME:

"It's a miracle."

"Oh, God, I have to go through labor again." —*Darcy, East Northport, New York*

"It's a miracle."

"This time I'm getting the right doctor."
—*Laurie, Phoenix, Arizona*

"It's a miracle."

"When will I sleep?"
—*Cynthia, Hollywood, Florida*

For many of us the second pregnancy is meticulously planned to fit into our lifestyles. There are fewer pure "accidents" with our second than with our first. Although there are some completely accidental second pregnancies, most second births are planned pregnancies. That child may come a bit earlier or a bit later, but the idea of a second baby is in the cards. In fact, in one study done by David Knox and Kenneth Wilson, professors of sociology at East Carolina University, almost half of the mothers surveyed (45 percent) reported that they had already decided when to have their second baby before they had even had their first!

Timing Is Everything

With a toddler or older child at home, most couples try to figure out the best time to add to their family. School teachers plan babies for the spring in order to have the summer off with their new family. Accountants may shoot for any time after April 15.

Others study the birth order books and try for their kids to be "ideally spaced" at 2.5 years apart. I know of sisters who planned each of their pregnancies together so that their kids would have each other to play with.

Finances also enter into the picture. Some couples feel the need to wait for the big bonus or the promotion before they try for number two. Studies show that the real dent in a family budget comes with the first child, and that the second child may cost only half as much in the beginning, considering the fact that many expenses such as cribs, car seats, strollers, and so on can be recycled with the second. However, having two children can still mean needing another bedroom, so saving for the bigger home or a house extension can also be a real consideration.

Some parents, on the other hand, just let their second child come along whenever it wants to. I envy people who are that relaxed. In my case, though, I was already plotting away in the maternity ward, nursing my daughter, Annie, and planning for what I thought would be the perfect time to have my second. I remember looking up the next two years in the back of my Filofax—how's that for anal retentive? In the end, it was all for naught; I ended up having my son, Alex, a bit earlier than planned—only eighteen months after Annie was born! So for a few moms like me, the second pregnancy comes as a bigger surprise than the first. "It took us four years to get pregnant with Tyler, so we just figured it would be a long time before I got pregnant again," says another mother with closely spaced children. "Then six months after Tyler, I got pregnant with Lindsay! It just shows you can't predict nature."

Birth Order

All parents have hopes, fantasies, and expectations about what their children will be like. Even without realizing it, you may already have tried to shape your firstborn's traits. You may want your daughter to be more assertive than you were or your son to become a leader in his Cub Scout troop. As an experienced parent of one, though, you probably have already figured out that you have very little control over what kind of personality your child will develop. While certain character traits are blamed on environment or "taking after" one parent or the other, often the real characteristics are attributed to either plain old genetics or to birth order.

Experts believe that the birth order and the spacing of your two children can directly influence what kind of people they become. Most parents will admit that even though they swear they raised both of their children the same way, they turned out as very different and unique people. The years between your children is another variable that shapes their personalities.

Age Spacing

Although some experts will tell you that there really is no such thing as ideally spaced siblings, parents do have opinions on this subject. According to a recent survey conducted by the Wirthin Group (affiliated with Ortho-McNeil Pharmaceutical) published in *Baby* magazine, 64 percent of women plan their families by spacing their children. And more than one thousand women polled say the ideal space between children is 2.5 years.

The latest study conducted by the Centers for Disease Control and Prevention shows that spacing your children two and a half years apart may be ideal for producing healthy, full-term babies. The study, conducted by Dr. Bao-Ping, and published in the February 1999 issue of *New England Journal of Medicine*, found that babies conceived within six months of their sibling had a 30 percent greater chance of being premature. Mothers who waited ten years before becoming pregnant again were twice as likely to have an unusually small baby or to deliver prematurely.

Joseph Rodgers, a professor at the University of Oklahoma, has done research in birth order and family size; and he points out that while he believes kids can adjust to any sibling birth order, there are a few generalities that can be made about their subsequent relationship.

"The closer two siblings are in age, the more likely they will both view themselves as friends as well as rivals," states Dr. Rodgers. "That's why so many parents complain about bickering and competing between their children. But the up side is that they are often very close with each other as a result of being so close in age."

"The bigger the age difference, the more likely the younger child will try to model himself after the older," he continues. "The older sibling can become a kind of hero to the younger."

In terms of sharing, Dr. Rogers divides age spacing into three general categories: (1) Children twelve to thirty-six months apart share friends, family, toys, and sometimes even playpens; (2) children three to six years apart share family, but not playmates or toys; and (3) children more than six or seven years apart have nothing in common until early adulthood.

My own theory, based on my relationship with my sister, born six years after me, is that although widely spaced siblings may practically ignore each other during childhood, they can become extremely close when they become adults. My sister and I actually began to get to know one another in our twenties. Now we speak on the phone at least once a day and plan our vacations together.

Frank Sulloway, a research scholar at the Massachusetts Institute of Technology and author of *Born to Rebel: Birth Order, Family Dynamics, & Creative Lives*, believes that birth order does matter greatly in determining human behavior. Here are some of his findings:

- Firstborns tend to be high achievers, assertive, and hard-working.
- Most female executives are firstborns.
- Firstborns are more respectful of authority. They pick up on what their parents value.
- Firstborns are less agreeable than later borns.
- Second children (with only one sibling) are more fun loving.
- Second children are more open to new experiences.
- Second children are more creative and more neurotic.

Remember, though, that knowing these traits will not automatically guarantee a certain kind of child. That is still in God's hands. In terms of timing your children's births, it is most important to consider your own needs. Many parents of two adult kids can look back on their child-rearing years and give what I believe is the best rule of thumb for spacing your children: Think about when you and your husband are emotionally and financially best ready to have another child. It will be better for you, your marriage, and your children.

One more study may be good to keep in mind. Robert B. Stewart, professor of psychology at Oakland University in Rochester, Michigan, reports in his book, *The Second Child: Family Transition and Adjustment*, that parents with closely spaced children wished that they had spaced them farther apart, and the parents with spaced children wished they'd spaced them closer! It may simply mean that given the degree of work involved with raising children, the grass may always seem greener on the other side of the fence. Whatever the spacing of your new family, you will find that just as no children are alike, no two pregnancies are alike either. The second time around can be even more exciting, overwhelming, terrifying, thrilling, exhilarating, and joyful than the first.

The Thrill of the
First Pregnancy . . . Remember?

We tend to go through our first pregnancy in some kind of dreamy haze. The thrill of it! Since we've never had a baby before, all we have to go on—besides the dozens of pregnancy books out there—is the powerful romantic images promoted by our culture. Remember the way TV shows used to handle pregnancy and childbirth? Mom goes into the hospital, smiling serenely in a wheelchair manned by silly, nervous Dad, and after the commercial Mom is being wheeled out of the hospital, holding a brand-new, perfect baby, still smiling serenely. (Thank God for the reality of Murphy Brown's pregnancy.) Even most films skirted around the issue—except in that scene in *Gone With the Wind* in which Melanie writhes in pain while Atlanta burns to the ground, but that was during the Civil War (I do have a friend who compares her experience of childbirth with that scene, however).

At any rate, the first pregnancy *does* feel like a kind of miracle. To me it felt like a religious experience—my husband and I had created a life! I was the first offspring pregnant on both sides of the family, so I had the added attention of grandparents, aunts, uncles, and cousins all focused on me. I had four baby showers in all. The stroller, the crib, the car seat, the diaper bag, the baby monitor, the electronic ear thermometer, the portable playpen, the hand-embroidered Christening outfit—I had it all. All my girlfriends wanted to go shopping for maternity clothes with me; and even though I didn't start to show until my fifth month, I began wearing those maternity jumpers at the beginning of my fourth. For nine months I felt as if I was the center of attention. My husband pampered me and even my high school English students seemed a little bit more accommodating. All in all, I felt like the star of the show.

This Time Around . . . Same Old,
Same Old?

I remember telling my mother I was pregnant with my second and her response was, "Ooh, that's wonderful . . . a playmate for Annie . . . how's her ear infection, by the way?" Well, so much for the miracle of life. While the announcement that you're pregnant again is greeted with congratulations, the news, in a way, is old news. Gone are the balloons and solicitude. Just when we really need some pampering—we're pregnant *and* we're taking care of our first—we find ourselves being slapped on the back and told, "Hey, you're an old pro now—you'll be fine!"

The second pregnancy has its advantages and disadvantages. The good part is that you've done it all before. The bad part is that you've done it all before. In other words, knowing what to expect can lower your anxiety (those "funny" kicks in your stomach, the mood swings) as well as increase it (another ten weeks of throwing up? another fifteen hours of labor?).

However, knowing what to expect the second time around is complicated by the fact that this time you are trying to care for your first child while getting ready for your second. That can be the single most difficult part of a second pregnancy. Mothers say:

> The OB-GYN appointments were the worst! I had no sitters available in the afternoon, so I'd lug Alexis in her baby seat into the office and ask the receptionist to watch her while I was in with my doctor. I couldn't even concentrate on the sonograms or my baby's heartbeat because I was so nervous over what Alexis was doing out there in the waiting room.   —Amy, *Sioux Falls, South Dakota*

My son was just great when I had morning sickness. We'd play "doctor," and he'd get me a damp washcloth when he heard me puking each morning. Then when I'd lie down, he'd lay it on my forehead and hold my hand. Believe it or not, I have fond memories of throwing up!

—*Corrine, Seattle, Washington*

What I remember is that I was just so damn tired all the time with my second pregnancy. With my first I slept late, napped in the afternoon, took bubble baths; with my second I was so exhausted taking care of my eighteen-month-old all day that I never had the time—or the energy—to worry or obsess over my pregnancy like I did with the first. It went by in a complete blur!

—*Nancy, San Diego, California*

What's Different About This Pregnancy?

Showing Early

"That was the biggest difference for me," says Kaily. "The first time I got pregnant I didn't start wearing maternity clothes until my fifth month. And even then I could have waited another few weeks. But when I got pregnant the second time, I found I couldn't button my jeans after the second month! I went right into stretch pants and my husband's shirts."

Many women find they're in a similar spot. This is believed to be true simply because our pelvic walls have already been stretched, so it's easier and faster to stretch again. Just think of the advantages of "easy stretch" when labor comes!

Finding Rest for a Pregnant Mom

Dr. Cassandra Henderson, an associate professor of obstetrics and gynecology at the Albert Einstein College of Medicine and Montefiore Medical Center in the Bronx, New York, notes that chronic and severe fatigue occur across the board in a second pregnancy. "Mothers who worked right up to the minute they delivered their first, for example, will simply not have the same energy the second time around." Stay-at-home moms who spent their first pregnancies taking naps and resting when they felt like it will not have that luxury again, says Henderson. Having a toddler or even an adolescent at home takes tremendous stamina, and she urges pregnant moms to prepare for fatigue as early on as possible. How to do that?

"Plug into family and community resources," Henderson states. "If you are without an extended family, find a teenager to come over after school to do some laundry and start dinner so that you can get off your feet for a bit." She adds that often this kind of help is just as important in the first trimester as in the last weeks.

Asking for help is hard for many of us. My very wise neighbor Betty, mother of four young adults, insisted that I rest more often and began taking Annie out of the house for an hour each Wednesday. I felt guilty at first, but by the third Wednesday, I had Annie dressed and in her stroller and was waiting for Betty at the screen door. That hour was heaven for me. Sometimes I just sat and opened the mail. Sometimes I played the piano, belting out show tunes off-key—not a pretty picture but oh, did it relax me. Once I watched an old episode of *Northern Exposure,* and once I spent the whole hour studying my stomach in the bedroom mirror.

I was lucky because someone offered. The second time someone asks, "Is there anything I can do . . . ?" take a deep breath and answer: "Well, it'd be great if you took my toddler in the stroller tomorrow afternoon!" There's nothing wrong with getting help when you need it. Ask neighbors, friends, members of your church or synagogue, and coworkers.

Swelling

Rest is one thing, resting the *right way* is another. Because we tend to be on our feet much more in a second pregnancy, it is especially important to elevate your legs as often as possible each day. The veins in your legs can swell due to the weight on your uterus. This condition is called varicose veins. (You can certainly have varicose veins without being pregnant.) Although a tendency toward varicose veins often is inherited and they can't be completely prevented, there are ways to relieve the discomfort. The American College of Obstetricians and Gynecologists suggests these tips to reduce edema:

- Rest in bed on your side.
- Recline with your legs raised on a small footstool or several pillows.
- Do not wear stockings or socks that have a tight band of elastic around the legs.
- If you must sit a lot on the job, stand up and move around from time to time.
- Try not to stand still for long periods of time.
- Don't cross your legs when you sit.

Rounding Up
the Usual Symptoms

You may have suspected you were pregnant earlier with this one than with your first. Your body is much more attuned to all the subtle changes going on, and many of the symptoms may seem familiar. However, with a second pregnancy some of these routine symptoms you're experiencing can shift a bit.

Morning Sickness

First the good news: Most mothers I have spoken with said that morning sickness during their second pregnancy was less severe than with their first. No one really knows why that is, but it seems to be true in most cases. With my first I had that ugh-I'm-getting-carsick-feeling for my first eight weeks. Although I never really threw up, I had saltines at my desk at school where I teach and several times I raced to the bathroom for false alarms. I dreaded repeating that with my second, but I needn't have worried. I had only a vague unsettled stomach for the first couple of weeks.

My friend Carol, a real estate attorney, agrees with this theory: "I was so sick with my first pregnancy that I used to travel with a box of Ziploc freezer bags in my briefcase—I never knew when I'd throw up. When I was pregnant with Maggie, though, I was down to once in the morning. So much better!"

Nurses and midwives are quick to point out this is not always the case. Although rare, it is possible to feel even worse during the second pregnancy. Most women I spoke to had stories similar to mine: However severe or slight their morning sickness was with their first pregnancy, it seemed markedly less so with their second.

Now the bad news: No matter how sick you get, you won't be able to take to your bed like the princess you were during your first pregnancy. You may have to "time" whatever vomiting you need to do because you will have your first child—in most cases a toddler or preschooler—following you right into the bathroom.

"I'd be hanging over the toilet and look up and see my two-year-old staring down at me with this look of horror on her face," says Alecia. "So naturally I had to calm her down at the same

time I was being sick. I learned I had to set the alarm an hour earlier each morning so I could throw up before my husband had to
leave for work—he'd try to occupy our daughter downstairs while
I was in the bathroom.

Breast Tenderness

Your breasts undergo changes from the very start of pregnancy in
order to prepare for nursing, so within the first six to eight weeks
you will probably notice them growing larger. However, with a
second pregnancy you may still be nursing your first when you
find out you're pregnant again. It is possible to continue nursing
your first during your second pregnancy, according to La Leche
League International, a nonprofit organization dedicated to helping nursing mothers. However, your firstborn may notice a change
in the taste of the milk due to the increased hormones, which
may cause the baby to back off a bit, or the baby may stop nursing
by the fourth month when the milk supply starts to decrease. By
the end of your second pregnancy, the milk changes to colostrum,
and the baby may wean entirely by then. La Leche League reports
that researchers found that 69 percent of nursing babies wean at
some time during their mother's subsequent pregnancy. If nursing
is an important part of your older baby's life, it is possible to continue nursing him or her along with your newborn.

Stretch Marks

If you got stretch marks on your stomach, buttocks, hips, or thighs
during your first pregnancy, it probably means you'll be getting
them with your second. There are several unsubstantiated beliefs
surrounding this phenomenon. Many women say that their
stretch marks seem darker with the second pregnancy, but again,
that is not true all the time. Another theory is that women with

darker complexions get darker stretch marks that don't fade as quickly or as completely as they do on those with fair skin. Stretch marks, however, as well as complexion tone itself, are directly influenced by genetics. Women who are prone to scarring are more likely to develop stretch marks. Also, if you developed stretch marks during puberty, for example, you are more likely to get them while pregnant. Other factors that contribute to stretch marks include skin elasticity and extreme weight gain during either pregnancy.

Frequent Urination

Oh yes, with the second pregnancy you will also have pressure on your bladder, so that you will once again need a bathroom every hour or so. In fact, your muscles may be a bit weaker after the birth of your first child, so you will be using unfamiliar restrooms everywhere. The Kegels exercises learned during your first pregnancy can be done now to help with this problem.

You may already have experienced those restrooms with your firstborn—especially if he or she has just recently been potty trained. How many of us have experienced those scary gas station bathrooms with our toddlers? My daughter used to wait until we were driving in bumper-to-bumper traffic on the expressway before she'd shout ominously from her car seat; "Potty, Mommy. Now."

My friend Sarah, who used to say she had to pee every twenty minutes during both pregnancies, thinks it was an advantage to ask for a bathroom when you have a little one in tow. "I'd always be too embarrassed to ask for the bathroom in an antique store or a small boutique—especially before I started to show in my second pregnancy. But when I was with my four-year-old, it was easy. I'd ask the clerk to use the restroom; and if she'd hesitate, I'd look down pointedly at Timmy and say, 'It's an emergency.' They'd get that key right out and open the bathroom."

A More Confident
Pregnant Mom

During my first pregnancy, I had a stack of pregnancy and child-birth books on my nighttable. It seemed that I was always frantic about one weird symptom or another. During my second, I still had weird symptoms, but I had lost that horrible panic about what was happening to my body.

"With my first," says Karen, mother of a one-year-old and a three-year-old, "I was on the telephone with my doctor every week. I'd go to my appointments with a notepad and ask a ton of questions. With my second, I hardly ever called him at all, and my appointments felt so routine."

In addition, those around us respect us a bit more, so there isn't that barrage of advice coming from everyone from doctors to the lady sitting next to us on the bus. We're also not so quick to swallow all the horror stories of pregnancy and childbirth some people feel compelled to tell us. It seems that all pregnant mothers have to endure Bad Labor Stories, the graphic details of endless labors so horrific it's a wonder any of us get pregnant at all. I remember being pregnant with our first and hearing a story about a woman who had such a hard labor that when she "pushed," all of her blood vessels burst in her face, and she ended up looking like W. C. Fields by the time she reached the maternity ward. Now I'm sure that never happened, but I carried that tale to the delivery room with me. When I was pregnant with Alex, however, I knew what to expect, more or less, and those grisly stories didn't hold as much power as before.

On the other hand, I had a whole new set of anxieties to focus on: How would this pregnancy be different from the first? What would be easier and what would be more difficult? I had, after all, done this once already; and I therefore had different anxieties with which to contend, the greatest of these looming in front of me from the start: What would *this* labor be like?

Our Bodies, Our Fears

Remembering the Labor from Hell

The odds are good that your second labor will be shorter. In fact, studies show that second labors are usually about half as long as first labors. No matter what the length, though, labor is the one part no one looks forward to. We often remember those most minute details because it is such a peak experience in our lives. For those of us who really had a tough time laboring with our first, the idea of going through it all again—even if we're told it will probably be shorter—is not only disheartening, but terrifying. And that terror can overshadow this pregnancy and possibly even ruin this otherwise happy time.

Pam England, a nurse-midwife and the author of *Birthing from Within: An Extra-Ordinary Guide to Childbirth*, works with pregnant mothers who have had a traumatic first birth and who, as a result, have very serious anxieties about their second labor and childbirth. She defines a "birth trauma" as any birthing experience that leaves a residual and negative memory. Of course, all childbirth is traumatic in and of itself, but England is referring to those women whose labors have been unusually long and painful, sometimes ending with a cesarean or other medical intervention that kept the mother from enjoying the actual birth. Often her patients remember their first birth as such a horrible experience that it has a bad effect on the second pregnancy. England suggests that with very deep trauma it is advisable to seek therapy before the second birth. That said, she encourages expectant moms to get back a sense of active control of their bodies. Here are some of her suggestions:

◆ If your bad experience could have been prevented by the hospital, write a letter of complaint to the person who offended you during your first birth. Send the letter to the administrator of the hospital. Avoid taking a victim approach; instead, indicate your dissatisfaction in a strong, assertive tone. You could certainly have had a bad experience without having anyone to blame for it, but when someone is to blame, letter writing is much more effective—for you as well as for future moms—than simply "standing around and complaining at parties about how horrible it all was," say England. Most hospitals have committees to investigate complaints, she adds, and getting a written response or sometimes even an apology goes a long way toward healing that trauma.

◆ Look inward and try to find the precise message you are telling yourself. "I'm just a wimp and can't take pain" and "Doctors can't be trusted" are two common phrases. Look for any exaggeration or overreaction you may be making and examine ways to redirect your own anxieties by actively looking for alternatives in this new pregnancy.

◆ Talk to your doctor or midwife. Explain your fears and ask specific questions relating to pain management. "Walk" through your previous labor with him or her, asking the person to suggest techniques or alternative methods to reassure you that the same events won't repeat themselves.

◆ Talk to mothers who have had more than one child about their own birthing experiences. Since second labors are historically easier, these birthing stories will be proof that just because you had one bad experience, you needn't repeat it a second time.

◆ Learn and practice relaxation techniques. A nurse-midwife can use art therapy to confront deep-seated fears. Many women have lowered their anxiety themselves with such methods as self-hypnosis and EMDR—eye movement desensitization reprocessing—a technique therapists use to bring about an awareness of our inner feelings relating to an incident.

Choosing a Practitioner

Will you be going back to your old doctor or midwife? One of the nice things about a second pregnancy is that it affords you the opportunity to look back on your whole birthing experience with an unjaundiced eye. By now you've swapped stories and anecdotes with other moms, and you probably have a pretty clear idea of what kind of experience you want this time around.

"I was *not* happy with the OB-GYN I had with my first baby. He was part of a highly regarded five-man practice, and although I liked him when I met him, I ended up seeing him only twice during my whole pregnancy. I hated my checkups because I never knew who'd be examining me. I felt as if no one even knew my name. I hadn't even met the doctor who delivered Ryan," says Dianne. "I decided to go with a nurse-midwife the second time around and was much happier."

On the other hand, you may have had a positive experience with your first pregnancy and may credit that to your practitioner. Some women who develop a close bond with their doctor during those nine months will want to continue that relationship in their second pregnancy:

"I love my doctor, and would never even consider switching to someone else. She knows me so well, knows my body and what it can and can't do, and I think that's a real advantage the second time around," says Edna. "Besides, I was able to say things to her that I couldn't say to anyone else. She answered my questions, she explained all my tests to me, she calmed me down when I got anxious, she even counseled me about my marriage. I trust her completely."

If you felt sort of neutral about your practitioner—you weren't thrilled with his techniques but you didn't really hate him, either—you may want to consider looking into other possibilities. After all, office visits tend to be even briefer with your second pregnancy. Everyone just assumes that you know the ropes, that your question were all answered the first time you were pregnant, so you may feel slightly neglected.

If it's been awhile since your first child was born, you may have lost touch with your doctor or midwife and may feel no particular attachment to him or her. In addition, new practitioners may have moved into your area, and new methods and techniques may have been developed since your last baby was born.

You are no longer automatically considered high risk if you are over thirty-five years old; but as you age, you may develop diabetes, anemia, or high blood pressure related to pregnancy. In addition, if your first child was born with any genetic disorders, you will naturally be concerned that it could happen again with your second. All these factors affect the very important decision about who you want to be your provider.

Another thing to consider is where you want to give birth this time. Were you satisfied with the hospital or birthing center? Often doctors make promises to their patients that the hospital will override at the time of the birth. For example, Karen's doctor promised to keep the "intervention" techniques down to a minimum during labor and childbirth, but the hospital's policy was to routinely use IVs and birth monitors during her labor. Although her doctor persisted on her behalf, Karen saw it as a sort of power struggle—something she clearly didn't need during her labor.

"The worst part came after I gave birth and was alone in the recovery room. This nurse walked in and said that if I didn't urinate within fifteen minutes, she'd be putting a catheter in!"

recalls Karen. "I tried to explain that I had just given birth fifteen minutes ago and needed a little time, but she was adamant. It was only when I insisted on speaking to my doctor that she backed off. And yes, I did manage to urinate a half hour later!"

Before you decide which obstetrician/gynecologist or nurse-midwife you'll use, think carefully about your first pregnancy and childbirth experience and try to isolate the area where you were the least happy.

- Were you comfortable with your doctor?
- Were your monthly or weekly appointments rushed?
- Did your provider fail to explain in understandable language the tests you had?
- Was the doctor at all condescending?
- Did you feel dumb asking certain questions?
- Did you feel as if the doctor was just patting you on the head and telling you to be a "good girl," or were you treated as a thinking adult?
- Was your doctor there for your labor, or did he or she magically appear in the delivery room?
- Did your doctor use unnecessary technical means?
- Was your doctor too quick to give you a cesarean, in your opinion?
- How was your doctor at pain management?
- Did your doctor insist on giving you an epidural before you were ready or did you have to beg for medication?
- Did you feel an episiotomy was necessary?
- How was the doctor's manner in the delivery room?

Once you have a handle on what you want to be different with this pregnancy, you can move on to decide whether you want to use an OB-GYN or a nurse-midwife. Each of these practitioners has a separate philosophy toward childbirth.

Obstetrician/Gynecologist

It is reassuring to use the same obstetrician if you've had a satisfactory experience the first time. You can both learn from the first pregnancy and find additional techniques to help you with your second labor and childbirth as well.

These physicians are trained to handle complicated, high-risk pregnancies as well as normal healthy-mom, garden-variety pregnancies. If you are thirty-five or older you will be offered an amniocentesis, and you will want clear answers concerning genetic counseling. If you've had previous miscarriages, you may feel more comfortable with an OB-GYN. (One in four pregnancies ends in miscarriage; studies show there is no greater risk in a second pregnancy if the first pregnancy ended in a miscarriage.)

Finding the right OB-GYN is not easy. Ask mothers who have given birth more than once for a solid recommendation. Go to the library and check into the physician's medical schooling and background. Find out what hospital he or she is affiliated with. Become reacquainted with your HMO group. Which doctors offer the best coverage? Your HMO group will also be able to supply you with a list of recommended physicians in your area. Does the doctor have a solitary practice, or does he or she work with other OB-GYNs? Who are the "backup" doctors and is there a possibility you will be given over to them without warning?

Even armed with this knowledge, it's hard to know what a doctor will be like. Without actually meeting a physician, how will you know whether or not his or her personality will jibe with yours? The next step, therefore, is to conduct an "interview." Call the doctor's office and ask to set up a free consultation. Years ago doctors would bristle at the thought of being interviewed. These days, however, it has become a common practice, and most OB-GYNs are amenable. Don't expect a long session, however. Count on ten or fifteen minutes, tops. So be prepared. Have a notebook listing specific questions you want answered. Here are some possible questions an *experienced* mother-to-be can ask:

- Do you treat second pregnancies any differently from firsts?
- How often do you schedule office visits for a second pregnancy?
- How long is each appointment?
- How many patients are scheduled for each appointment block of time?
- Is there a certain time of the day when you take phone calls from patients?
- If I bring my toddler with me to your office, is there someone who can watch him or her during my appointment? Can I bring my toddler into the examining room with me?
- How do you define a high-risk pregnancy?
- What is your cesarean rate?
- What is your VBAC (vaginal birth after a cesarean) rate? (See chapter 5.)
- Do you do routine episiotomies? If so, why?
- Can my child be in the labor room and the delivery room?
- Can my child visit me in the maternity ward?
- Do you accept birth or labor plans? (These plans are a kind of manifesto the patient writes up to indicate what kind of labor she prefers. For example: no IV, certain pain medications, being allowed to walk around during labor, and so on.) (See chapter 7.)

Listen closely to the doctor's responses. Are your questions answered clearly and without condescension? Watch the doctor's body language. Does the doctor seem to have time for you now or is the doctor's hand on the doorknob as he or she responds?

Finally, trust your instincts. Do you like him or her? Is this doctor someone you want to have delivering your baby?

Nurse-Midwife

It was really after my second birth that I learned about midwifery. A woman I'd met in my mothers' group had used a midwife for her second birth and had absolutely raved about her experience. In Cathy's case, she had had an emergency cesarean section with her first child, but had felt it was an unnecessary procedure. She had also been hooked up to a fetal monitor and IV during all of her labor, which meant she was unable to leave the hospital bed and move around for over eight hours. She felt "disconnected" during the C-section and had vowed to have a vaginal birth with her second. Although it took some researching, she found a nurse-midwife affiliated with her local hospital. Her midwife had spent a great deal of time with her during her office visits, and Cathy felt that the added support was just what she needed. Because her midwife had taken the time and effort to get to know her as a person, Cathy was able to voice her fears and concerns in a manner she had felt unable to do with a medical doctor. She gave birth vaginally the second time around without any medical intervention in one of the hospital's new birthing rooms.

Once commonplace in both rural and urban areas, midwifery declined in developed countries after World War II, at about the same time formula started to replace breast milk and mothers were "put under." My own mother was medicated when I was born in the 1950s. But in the 1970s, with the rise of feminism, women began taking a more active role in their own health. Women's groups demanded that fathers be allowed in the delivery room, for example, and some were requesting home births with less routine technology used in labors. Midwifery started to make a marked comeback, and it has been gaining steadily in popularity, especially within the last ten years. The National Center for Health Statistics reported that in 1995, 6 percent of all U.S. births were delivered by certified nurse-midwives, compared with 3 percent in 1989. Now many HMOs cover midwifery, and most hospitals also accept accredited midwives.

The work *midwife* means simply "with woman," and that is really the short answer to what a midwife does as opposed to a traditional OB-GYN. Educated first as a nurse, then trained in a two-year midwifery program that grants a master's degree, a midwife "stays" with the expectant mother until the baby is born. That does not mean that she lives with the mother during this time; it simply means she is much more accessible than a traditional OB-GYN would be. Midwives generally stay with the mother during most or all of her labor. A midwife can work in tandem with a physician, especially in the case of a high-risk pregnancy or complicated birth, or she can work alone, seeing patients for their monthly and weekly checkups and handling the delivery herself.

According to the American College of Nurse-Midwives (ACNM), all certified nurse-midwives have physicians on call. Roughly 95 percent of midwife-assisted deliveries take place in a hospital, with 5 percent delivered at home.

In many ways, the main difference between a midwife and an OB-GYN is one of philosophy. Kay Sedler, administrator and chief of the Midwifery Division at the New Mexico University School of Medicine, sees the role of the nurse-midwife as one that focuses on the choices available to a healthy pregnant woman. "We try to address the concerns of the mother by spending more time with her and incorporating a more holistic approach to prenatal care, with less medical intervention." For example, midwives will work with a laboring mother to find her most comfortable position. That may be on her hands and knees on the floor, in the bathtub, or pacing back and forth. Most midwives believe that a routine episiotomy is usually unnecessary, and that a "tear" is preferable to an incision. Indeed, tears can often be prevented with the use of oils and massage, and the vagina can be "taught" to stretch to accommodate the head of the infant. "But these techniques require time," cautions Sedler. "Most physicians cannot or will not take that time."

"Physicians," Sedler believes, "are trained to focus on technology, on serious medical problems. With a healthy pregnant woman who does not have problems and proceeds as expected, these doctors are not quite as engaged. As a result, I don't think they have the patience to address the common fears and questions most women have at this time."

Sedler suggests that pregnant moms participate in much the same interview process as they would with perspective OB-GYNs. Here are some additional questions to ask a nurse-midwife:

- "What is your philosophy on labor for a healthy pregnant mother?"
- "What hospital and what physicians are you affiliated with?"
- "What tests can you administer?"
- "Does my HMO cover midwifery?"
- "At what point in a difficult delivery would you involve a physician?"
- "What percentage of your deliveries have had to involve a physician?"

What Is a *Doula*?

A *doula* is a woman who, in addition to the nurse-midwife or doctor, stays with the mother during labor, childbirth, and/or postpartum. This practice has become popular recently, it is believed, because fewer women have the support of their extended family. Parents and aunts and uncles move away, sisters are working full time, and no one seems to have the time to help the new mom.

According to Marion McCartney, executive director of the College of Nurse-Midwives in Washington, D.C., there are two ways a *doula* can function. One is simply as a "warm, constant female presence whose sole job is to be with the mother during her labor, childbirth, and postpartum." The second is during the postpartum time only (see chapter 7). She may come to the house for several hours a day for a week or longer to be a support to the mother. Her job is not to feed or care for the newborn, but to care for the mom. "The *doula* often functions as a good friend," explains McCartney, "or as substitute for her extended family. She may help with a few household chores, or help the mother to breast-feed." *Doulas* are not licensed, since they are not there to give medical care, so the best way to locate a *doula* is through your childbirth educators, breast-feeding organizations such as La Leche League, or even through your local hospitals, which are starting to list recommended *doulas* (see chapter 7).

Guilt and the Pregnant Mom

"I felt so guilty during my second pregnancy," admits Vicki. "I was so busy dealing with my firstborn's adjustment to preschool that I hardly paid any attention to my baby's kicks or making sure I was eating the right amount of broccoli and orange juice. I even lost the photo of his first sonogram."

"I felt so guilty during my second pregnancy," admits Risa. "I was so busy obsessing over my test results, especially my amniocentesis, that I hardly paid any attention to my seven-year-old daughter. I skipped parent conferences and didn't chaperone her field trips that year, but I just couldn't focus on her while I was pregnant."

It just goes to show that a pregnant mom can't win! Even those moms able to keep a sense of perspective with their firstborn and not-quite-born often feel guilty about ignoring their husbands or women friends or parents or in-laws or bosses. The list is endless. It's important to know that all these feelings are pretty normal and also to realize that you are being pulled in many directions and that it is up to you to try to be a little bit kinder to yourself emotionally during this time. It's even more important to understand that feeling guilty is completely normal during a second pregnancy—especially during those last few weeks when emotions seem to spiral downward into chaos.

To control those feelings of guilt, Tony Jurich, Ph.D., president of the American Association for Marriage and Family Therapy and professor of family studies at Kansas State University, suggests that expectant moms make two "contacts" during their pregnancy:

"First, find someone you really trust—it can be your husband or your sister or your best friend—and release those feelings: the fears, the guilt, the middle-of-the-night demons. The other person doesn't have to offer advice; they just have to listen. It sounds like a cliché, but talking about it is the first and most important way to let go of the stress and lighten the load.

"Second, find someone who has gone through the same experience and has two—or even three or four—children." Jurich suggests approaching a neighbor, a coworker, your mother, or a friend, and opening with something like: "Am I crazy, or did you go through this too?" It's so important to understand that you are not going through some strange aberration of nature. Once you talk to others who've survived this experience, he says, "you will realize you are just another pulse in the heartbeat of life."

Can I Stretch My Love to Two?

Many moms worry that the intense and all-consuming love they feel for their first child can never be "stretched" to include an additional baby. Yet mothers of two kids agree that a mother's love knows no limits.

"I worried that I would just not have enough love left over," admitted Melanie. "But I found a mother's love is so bountiful that new love sort of just sprouts up." Sueann explains it this way: "It isn't that you love more or less or better or worse with your second child. You just love *different*. The love is every bit as powerful; it's just different."

⊰ TIPS FROM THE TRENCHES ⊱

✦ As soon as you find out you're pregnant, start looking into your maternity leave and disability policies at work. Sometimes companies are flexible about breaking up your leave time into two or more blocks. At the time I was trying to wean my two-year-old, I also had awful morning sickness, so I was able to take part of my leave during the first month of my second pregnancy when I really needed it. —*Cathy, Fort Salonga, New York*

✦ My mother-in-law gave me a wonderful shower present when I was expecting my first: a "day of beauty" at a local spa. I got a facial, a haircut, a manicure, and a pedicure, which really cheered me up in the last weeks of pregnancy. With my second, naturally, I got no presents like that, but I did remember how good it had made me feel. So I made another appointment for the week before I was due, and this time, knowing from the experience that it'd be months before I could take care of myself again, I threw in an eyebrow waxing and shoulder massage! —*Clare, Santa Ana, California*

❖ Take a refresher course in Lamaze or other childbirth class. Even just one session will help you remember how to breathe. Besides, new techniques may have been developed since your last childbirth. Also, get a baby-sitter and bring your husband with you, and then go out to dinner or to a movie to "celebrate" your good fortune.   —*Debbie, Salt Lake City, Utah*

2

Preparing Your Marriage

I felt like I was losing my husband. I had been the one to push for a second child before he thought we were ready financially. He had started working a second job when our first was born, and I was working full-time too. I was also trying to spend more time with our three-year-old before the new baby came along. My husband felt totally abandoned, I think. He would come home from work and say things like, "If this is the way it is with one, what's going to happen to us with two?" My stress level was off the Richter scale.

—*Gloria, Trenton, New Jersey*

During my second pregnancy my husband sort of started to detach. He would spend his weekends in his garage workshop, making "projects"—repairing the old crib, extra closet stuff—supposedly to prepare for the new baby, but it felt like he was really hiding out there and avoiding me and our two-year-old. —*Joanna, Carle Place, New York*

Both of us were just so tense during my second pregnancy. When our first was born we didn't cope very well; we had awful memories of arguing and sleep deprivation and just all that custodial work. I think we were both dreading going through it all over again.   —*Madeline, Olympia, Washington*

Yes, it is true that a second child can be the greatest stress test to a marriage. What, you say? You may be thinking that the big change in your marriage came after the birth of your *first* child. Like your lifestyle doing an abrupt 360-degree turn the day you came home from the hospital with your tiny bundle of joy. No more sleeping late—actually, no more *sleeping!*—no more spontaneous sex, no more leisurely dinners. Okay, you've adjusted to all that. How much change could another child bring?

Elizabeth Ellis, Ph.D., clinical psychologist and author of *Raising a Responsible Child*, gives seminars on how to cope to new mothers at Gwinnett Medical Center in Atlanta. She asks her clients to imagine their marriage as two people with a circle around them. The circle forms boundaries from others and protects them from the outside world. "Without children, all their time and energy is focused on each other," Ellis states. "When a woman becomes pregnant, she begins to detach from her husband and especially in the last few weeks. She focuses all her attention on her about-to-be-born baby. Suddenly she is uninterested in her spouse. She couldn't care less that he had a bad day or needs a new pair of pajamas. Instead she's concentrating on her changing body and her upcoming labor."

Ellis explains that once the baby is born, that circle has to open up to become a family unit of three. The role of each spouse has to change and shift in order to let in the child. Now the focus centers around the baby, who is completely helpless and in need of constant care. This is when biology takes over. "Eventually, husband and wife come to some accommodation. They manage to still make time for each other, although not as much time as when they were childless." Still, one child is manageable, she notes. Ellis, a mother of two, remembers the days after her oldest was born as a time when she and her husband were at least able to shift the duties of parenting back and forth. "My husband would make a telephone call while I held the baby. I'd take a shower while my husband fed the baby. There was always time for one another when the baby was asleep," she says. "But when our second was born, we couldn't trade off duties—each of us had a child—and the time alone together was shortened to 'when both babies were asleep at the same time,' which wasn't very often!"

Furthermore, she explains, "When the second child comes along, that circle is opened even wider, and that means renegotiating all the roles and relationships toward each other again. Those reciprocal roles of 'what I give' and 'what you give,' need to be revised."

Don and Iris experienced that widening circle as their family grew. "After our first was born," says Iris, "my husband I were overwhelmed by the responsibility. For a while we stopped relating to each other at all. All of our attention went to the baby."

Her husband, Don, agrees. "I remember going into the nursery in the middle of the night and just watching Kyle sleep. Was he still breathing? That's where we were for the first few months, and he was a completely healthy, normal newborn!"

By the time Iris and Don were expecting their second, Kyle had turned three; and while they were still interested in his breathing, they had begun to relax a bit. Things were getting back to normal. "Our marriage felt like a rubber band," Iris remembers. "It had stretched out a lot during those first couple of years; there was some tension and adjustments we both had to make, but then it seemed to bounce back and we sort of settled into a nice relationship again. Our sex life started to pick up, we were using baby-sitters and went out a few times a month, and we were able to take Kyle with us a lot. If we went to a museum in the afternoon, we'd sort of take turns keeping him occupied. We were tired but we managed to find time for us."

"Then Kristen was born," interrupts Don. "That was when all hell broke loose. We found the parenting strategies that worked with Kyle didn't work with Kristen. Lugging two kids around was just too hard, so we stayed home more. Also, our personal lives sort of disappeared for a while. Everything was chaos. And, as a result, our relationship really suffered."

The "Second Child" Marital Hurdles

Like Don and Iris, most couples wonder why the second baby throws a household into such disorder. After all, we've all done it before, yet the second time seems so much more difficult! Statistics go along with couples' experiences. Most studies show that the toughest year in a marriage is after the birth of the *second* child.

What is it about adding another child that makes married life so much tougher? There seem to be several reasons for this phenomenon. After your second baby:

Fatigue Is Greater

Just think of all the things you both do now for your firstborn, and then add all the things you had to do when he was a newborn, then put them together. That's a typical day when you have two kids. Added to that is your marriage. Now how do you and your husband feel about having wild nights of sexual experimentation? Being too tired for romance is just one hurdle that tends to erode the intimacy in a relationship. The more tired you are, the less patient you become, so that the smallest disagreements can become major fights.

"I remember—after a night of breast-feeding my newborn every two hours and doling out baby Tylenol for my two-year-old's fever—watching my husband put his coffee cup on the counter instead of rinsing it out and placing it in the dishwasher. I completely lost it. I yelled and wept; I carried on as if he had assaulted me. Now *that's* fatigue," recalls Lydia. "He, in turn, got mad at me for overreacting. I don't think we spoke to each other for three days." Lydia looks back on the event with a rueful smile, but acknowledges that at the time it was unpleasant and hurtful.

Finances Are Tighter

Studies show that it costs less to raise the second child than it does to raise the first, mainly because you've already bought the expensive stuff: the crib, the stroller, the car seat, the playpen, the clothes, the high chair, the swing-o-matic, the child-proofing gates and other paraphernalia needed with a little one. It is assumed a parent can use the items for their second, third, and fourth children. There's just one problem. Many children are closely spaced and therefore parents need to buy seconds. For example, in most states a child is now required by law to be outfitted with a car seat until age five. If baby number two arrives before baby number one reaches five, it's back to Toys "R" Us for another car seat. That goes for a stroller, too—even six-year-olds get tired of walking in the park and need to take a load off for a while. So that means getting another stroller or even a double stroller.

In addition, space becomes an issue with another baby; another bedroom may be needed. This is the time many parents opt for moving into a larger house or adding a costly addition to their existing home. Suddenly with two kids, a "playroom" becomes desirable. "We just had to expand; two kids in the living room was a disaster. There was no place for adults! We had our basement finished so that the kids could have their own play area. As expensive as it was, it was necessary to keep our own sanity," one father explains.

There are other less direct costs involved. If one parent—usually the mother—decides that day care will be too expensive for two, she might give up her salary to stay home with her children. In defining expenses in raising a family, the Population Reference Bureau in Washington, D.C., calls this expense an "opportunity cost" because there is the additional loss of the opportunity for a future salary. To make up for this loss of salary, the spouse may take on a second job or work longer hours to make more money. This gives the couple even less time together.

This drain on the budget means there is less money to spend on smoothing out marital stress. Where before, couples might splurge on a restaurant or other night on the town to regain their romance, they now may have to settle for a pizza and a rented video. In addition, all those extras both partners spend on themselves and each other, such as clothes, makeup, facials, and health club memberships, which make them feel good and sexy and desirable, are often curtailed.

The Workload Is Heavier

Taking care of two children requires an almost Herculean effort on the part of both mom and dad. However, many, many, many mothers complain that most of the custodial care falls on their shoulders. Some fathers respond by saying that they bring home a paycheck and that that should count for something. Providing for your family does, of course, count, yet these differences of opinion can erode a relationship. "One of our favorite 'fight topics'" states Sally, "is about who does more work and what work is most valuable. It never solves anything, but it shows how resentful we both are."

In fact, studies show that when both partners are surveyed on specific custodial chores such as house cleaning, yard work, repairs, caring for baby and older sibling, laundry, and meal preparation, each thinks he or she contributes more than the other. However, it is difficult to actually identify all the "jobs" we do for our children. For example, many women feel they do "invisible" work that their husbands don't even notice: the scheduling of play dates, pediatrician appointments, swimming lessons, and the like, as well as extra jobs such as baking brownies for class parties, writing out thank-you cards, and attending parent conferences.

"I am the brains of the outfit in our family," says Marissa. "My husband has no idea how long I spend on the phone just organizing our life. When Bobby is invited to a birthday party, my husband thinks he'd really 'working' by dropping him off at the party on his way to play golf. And I do appreciate his doing that. But he doesn't think of what I did: shop for the gift, buy a card and wrapping paper, wrap the gift, look for tape, look for ribbon, get Bobbie to address the card, make sure Bobbie has on a clean shirt."

Donna feels especially burdened as a working mother: "I work alongside my husband at our dry-cleaning business, but at the end of the day, he sits down with a beer while I help the kids with homework, talk to the day care woman, then make dinner. He loads the dishwasher afterward, yes, but I feel like I do everything else."

Yet it seems in recent years many fathers are doing more housework and child care—especially after the birth of their second child.

"My wife and I both work, so when we come home we each take a kid and spend one-on-one with him," says Tom. His wife adds, "It was easier before we had our second—back then we'd take turns 'chilling' with the newspaper. But these days we try to divide just about everything down the line—otherwise we end up feeling put-upon."

Time Is Shorter

"That's an understatement," says David, father of two girls. "There is *no* time for each other because every minute of the day revolves around our two daughters." He adds that there just seems to be so much more effort and time needed to raise kids nowadays than when he was a child. "My wife drives our seven-year-old to ballet on Wednesdays, piano on Thursdays, and religious instruction on Mondays. I'm the soccer coach, so there goes our weekends. Our youngest is going to Gymboree one day, a play date another. We're lucky if we all eat dinner together!" he explains. "Both of us also teach school, so after the kids are in bed we're grading papers and trying to decompress. Any time we have left over is spent sleeping, not fooling around!"

Everything seems to take more time with two children. One study showed that 76 percent of mothers surveyed reported that they had less time for themselves after their second child was born. They cited the constant interruptions, the "sick call duty," and the custodial care, such as doing laundry and meals. Fathers are also busier—if not earning extra money then by occupying the oldest while the youngest is being nursed or by bathing the youngest while mom helps the oldest with his or her homework. Time is also spent solving problems and settling differences between the two siblings. When the new baby arrives, the older child may regress a bit, so additional time and effort need to be spent giving him or her extra attention to compensate for the spotlight focused on the newborn.

Two children means more time spent arranging play dates, talking to preschool teachers, more piano recitals, more sports activities . . . the list is endless. And as wonderful as it is for parents to watch their children grow and mature during all these activities, it means less time for each other.

Parents Have Different Child-Rearing Techniques

In addition to all the above threats to a marriage, there comes the added challenge of knowing you will be raising another child. Already you may have noticed a conflict with your husband over the raising of your firstborn. Differing child-rearing methods begin to show up early on, and rarely do parents agree on every aspect of child rearing: "Should we let Johnny cry all night or should we let him sleep in our bed with us?"; "Can preschooler Susie learn to tie her own shoes now, or does it really make any difference if Daddy does it?"

The arrival of the second child increases the spotlight wattage on parenting techniques even more. Both parents now need to care for two children. Even in cases where couples have taken on traditional roles—Mom stays home and raises the kids while Dad works—fathers tend to become much more involved with parenting with their second child by reason of sheer need. That means, in all probability, two different disciplinary styles. After all, you and your spouse were raised in different families—whether you were an only child or the youngest of five, whether your mother was a strict parent or your father was, whether your parents were demonstrative and affectionate or were more distant—all these parenting styles in your own childhood influence how you will respond to your own children. Displaying the ideal "united front" becomes more difficult with two.

Holding On to the "Marital Thread"

Marriages certainly do shift even more after the birth of the second child. In fact, in a recent study, researchers found that couples with one child were more likely to describe their marriage as a "romance," while couples with two children tended to describe theirs as a "partnership."

Somehow, parents must find time for one another even as they approach the busiest years of their marriage. Certainly much of the anxiety during a second pregnancy—on the part of both husband and wife—comes from the fear that there will be no energy left over for each other once the new baby arrives. Already with only one child they've seen a big shift in their relationship. How will they keep their "coupleness" in the face of two kids?

"First, couples should take specific measures—now, during the second pregnancy—to keep their relationship thriving so that once the second child is born they will have already built-in strategies to sort of 'find' each other amid the diapers and the 3:00 A.M. feedings," states William Pinsoff, Ph.D., clinical psychologist and president of the Family Institute at Northwestern University. "The day-to-day business of raising two children can certainly fragment a marriage if couples don't take an active role in keeping that marital thread just as strong as the parenting thread," he cautions. He adds that some of the strategies the couple used to reconnect after the birth of their first child may not be possible during a second pregnancy or after the birth of the second child because there is less time and fatigue is so much greater. Here are his suggestions for keeping couplehood:

Make "Dates"

"Reserve time one night a weekend and one night during the week that is devoted solely to each other," offers Pinsoff. He adds that the only way couples are assured of having time together is if they get out the calendar and plan ahead for a date. It doesn't sound very romantic, does it? But pregnant couples need to make a small adjustment in that area. Romance is a relative term once you become a parent. Knowing that on Tuesday night at 7:00 P.M.

you and your husband have an "ice cream date" can be just as thrilling after a day of caring for a newborn and a toddler, for example, as dining at a French restaurant was *before* you became a mother.

Here are a few guidelines for successful dates:

◆ Make a habit of getting out the calendar on Sunday night and looking over the week's itinerary. Pick a weekday and weekend day and time for each other right then and there. If you don't write it down it will get lost in the litany of other "more important" appointments. List the specifics on the calendar such as "Wednesday 7:00–8:30: Walk to beach," for example.

◆ If baby-sitters are not available and/or too expensive, make a deal with your neighbor or a friend and take turns looking after each other's children. Use your in-laws and other extended family, even if you hate to ask for favors. Some couples find it difficult to ask others to look after their kids "for no good reason." "I felt dumb asking my mother-in-law to watch Frannie so Bill and I could have a date, so instead I said we had to do errands," says one mom. "Now it's become a regular Thursday appointment—she knows that's the day we drop off Frannie to do 'errands'—although I'm sure she suspects we're not really picking up the dry cleaning or going grocery shopping!"

◆ The "date" does not have to be expensive or long in duration. Even one hour alone together can ease the emotional pressures of parenting. A drive to Starbucks or to the yogurt store can be a way of reconnecting as a couple. Avoid going to the movies or other spectator activities. A walk through your neighborhood, a picnic, a trip to an arboretum, for example, encourage a relaxed atmosphere, which in turn promotes communication. It's best to get away from your stressful environment—i.e., your house—but I know of some couples who drop off their kids at the baby-sitter's

and then come back to the house to relax in front of the fireplace
or sit in the garden as a kind of home-without-the-noise vacation.

• No talking about the offspring. Before we had kids, my husband and I discussed the consistency of his pasta primavera; after
we had kids, we discussed the consistency of our children's bowel
movements. Too hard? Too stringy? Too green?

It's hard, believe me, to pull your focus onto each other after a
day with children, but it can be done. Even these days, when
we're trying to concentrate on each other, we automatically start
every sentence with a kid reference: "Mmm, delicious yogurt," my
husband will begin. "Oh look, they have peanut butter yogurt today—Annie's favorite."

"Oh, yeah," I'll say, "but I don't think she should have all that
dairy, do you?"

"Well, it doesn't seem to bother Alex, but Annie might be lac-
tose intolerant."

You get the idea. It usually takes us several false starts before
we can even *think* about something else. The point is that eventually we do, and that's when we turn into a couple again. There
is certainly nothing wrong with couples discussing their kids, but
during your scheduled time together try to find other topics to
talk about. If your mind's a blank, try starting with a memory you
shared from your "early days" or brainstorm some topics that both
of you can use to get the ball rolling.

• No double-dating. As tempting as it might be to invite another couple to join you, make it a rule that it be just the two of
you. "Going out with friends does nothing for your marriage,"
states Pinsoff. "It just serves to take the focus off the two of you.
This is the time to devote solely to each other—to protect your
marriage. There will be other times to socialize."

Handling It Better
the Second Time Around

Before we had kids, my husband and I had this idyllic, loving relationship. We'd leave little notes for each other at work, we'd snuggle up with the newspapers and each other on Sunday mornings, we'd take off on last-minute weekend trips whenever we felt like it. When we decided to have kids, we thought our marriage was so solid *nothing* could interfere with it. But we had not figured on the power of a baby. I had read everything I could find on the subject, but alas, I was still not prepared. Neither was my husband.

When our first was born, we really had a terrible meltdown—fights, tension, screaming at each other in the middle of the night when the baby wouldn't stop crying. We each felt we were doing much more work than the other, and suddenly we each felt completely unloved. Gone was the closeness we had felt before we had kids. It seemed as if days went by without our looking into each other's eyes. We each held on to our own resentments until one of us exploded over some small thing. It took us a long time to adjust to our new life; and when we found out I was expecting another baby, we knew we had to prepare for this one much more carefully in order to preserve our relationship.

Many couples go through the first child trial-by-fire syndrome and the thought of going through it all over again creates extreme tension for them both. What can we do for each other to prepare us for next time?

Darcy Pattison, C.S.W., and therapist with Family and Child Guidance Associates in Deere Park, N.Y., uses a number of techniques to prepare couples for their second child. "Toward the end of the second pregnancy, couples need to reevaluate their relationship. What do they see as their roles now that they are parents? What do they foresee as potential problems once the new baby comes along? What, specifically, breeds anger and resentment? And most importantly, what strategies worked and what didn't work with their first?" To help couples remain connected to each other emotionally, especially during the early weeks and months of second-time parenthood, Pattison suggests the following:

• Set aside time to sit down together and discuss your roles as parents and as partners and then note your levels of satisfaction and disappointment the first time around. Choose a neutral spot—a restaurant or, if at home, the living room or picnic table outside in your yard where you are more likely to be calm and less argumentative.

• Take a couple of days for each of you to come up with your own personal list—two columns—of what you think your spouse did right and wrong during that postbaby time. (Don't discuss or show him the list while you are composing.) But try to remember details that would help the other person see your side. Try to describe your feelings without casting blame on the other person. Although it's impossible to do all the time, a good method is to start your "feelings" comments with "I" so instead of writing, "You're such a slob," you write, "I feel so overwhelmed when I look at your clothes on the floor while I'm breast-feeding."

A wife might write: "It helped me when you threw in a load of laundry before you went to work," or "You used to pretend to be asleep when the baby cried in the middle of the night, and I hated you for that." A husband might write: "You used to wait for me at the screen door with our crying baby in your arms, hand him over, and moan, 'Now I can take a shower.' I'd never even have a chance to take off my coat!" or "Once in a while if the baby was asleep and I brought in take-out, you'd light the candles—that made me feel we were still a couple." When both of you have finished your lists, set aside a night to get together again.

• Meet in that same neutral place—maybe with a glass of wine—and then exchange lists. Read your spouse's list silently without comment. Are you surprised at what your spouse wrote? Were there similarities with what you wrote? Don't be discouraged if the "what you did wrong" column is longer than the "what you did right" column. Now discuss each other's lists. What can each of you do next time to improve your relationship? Talk about areas you think will pose potential problems. For example, how will you both handle the bedtime routine when the new baby is born? Often it takes both parents to put one child to sleep. Will you trade off duties? How about mealtimes? If you will be nursing, will your husband know that at that moment he needs to occupy your oldest? Spend a few moments talking about your own childhoods and what you might have missed as a child. Did you feel abandoned by your mom when your younger brother was born? Did your dad seem to "disappear" because he was working a double shift? Thinking about these experiences may make you more sensitive to your own parenting issues.

• Once you have a general understanding of each other's needs, Pattison says, it is time to make a joint list. "You and your husband are creating a visual image—a kind of blueprint—for keeping the relationship strong during this upcoming time when your children are so needy. The goal is to find ways to bring pleasure to your partner." These "random acts of kindness" may include such small, seemingly minor acts as bringing home a spouse's favorite old movie on video, or running the bath for one another, or offering a foot massage at the end of a long day. The list can go into effect now, while you're pregnant, as a trial run.

Pattison points out that the list serves as a tool to connect the parent's fantasy with reality. For example, "I know it sounds silly, but I really feel loved when you put a note in my lunch box," one father might admit. "When my sister calls long distance, I love it when you take the baby outside so we can talk."

• Put the list in a special, private place. Refer to it at times when you're feeling frustrated or overwhelmed, or when you think your spouse may be at the end of his or her rope. For example, your husband comes home late after working overtime and fighting traffic only to find you dealing with a teething infant, a three-year-old and her potty accident, and a broken washing machine. This is the moment to get out the list and find something—anything—you can each do for the other person to let them know that despite everything, you are still a loving couple.

Sex and the Pregnant Parent

Speaking of being loved, there is nothing that sparks the love factor so much as indulging in a healthy sex life. Just ask any man. Husbands are included under this heading, even if they are about to become fathers a second time around. Maybe *because* of that point, it is worthwhile to look into the notion of your sexual relationship during your second pregnancy.

There's no doubt that a couple's sex life takes a marked curve downward once they have a baby. It's always rich in irony to note that although the addition of two children ultimately brings the two of you the closest emotionally, they are also responsible for keeping you apart physically—at least for a while. The reasons, by now, should be pretty obvious to you and your husband. Remember back to the birth of your firstborn. Even if you were one of the lucky ones who experienced an increase in sexual appetite during your first pregnancy and managed to maintain incredible self-esteem while topping the scale at two hundred pounds—you probably lost that spark once you turned Mother.

In addition to hormones, biology, and too much focusing on your baby, plain old fatigue and time constraints play a huge part in a couple's decreased time in bed. As my cousin admitted, "There's something weird about having sex now that you're somebody's parents. You kind of lose the old razzle-dazzle."

Unfortunately, a second pregnancy tends to diminish the sex drive even further—one survey showed that only a third of expectant parents had sex more than once a week, and that by the time the mothers reached their third trimester, one in five stopped having sex altogether. As depressing as these statistics are, it's important to add that it can get better once you settle into life as parents of two children. Dr. Pinsoff offers some guidelines for improving your sexual relationship.

Get to Bed Early

Despite the myriad nightly chores, like making lunches and laying out clothes and reading bedtime stories, couples who make it a habit to turn in for the evening together at an early hour tend to be more prone to become intimate. But not right away, adds Pinsoff. "Lying down in bed is often the first *nondemanding* moment of the day. Couples need at least fifteen minutes to decompress. But if they retire early, then sex at least becomes a possibility before sleep."

Keep the Kids in Their Own Bed

"I am not an advocate of the 'family bed,'" states Pinsoff. "It discourages intimacy between couples and it rejects necessary boundaries between parents and children. There's nothing wrong with children knowing Mom and Dad are having private time."

He suggests that if kids come into your bedroom at night due to a nightmare or other interruption, walk or carry them back to their bed and sit with them there for a few moments.

Get the TV Out of the Bedroom

We all know TV is a distraction—that's why we are so careful to limit it with our children. It would be a wise idea to take our own advice. Watching television causes us all to fall into a vegetative state. Without it, couples may be forced (gently!) to focus on each other.

Resolve Your Anger

"Two people with two kids are going to get angry in their daily life. There's no getting around it. However, if it's allowed to fester unresolved, it keeps couples from being close," state Pinsoff. He suggests that if necessary, couples *use* the anger as a basis for connecting, for lively communication.

Personally, I recommend the following: Strike while the iron's hot! That is, when that rare moment comes when both kids are actually asleep at the same time—be it naptime or bedtime—that is the time to try for a few moments of intimacy. And, of course, it may only be a few moments—most parents have learned to pare down the Act to just the necessary stuff. My husband and I have learned to work ourselves into a sexual frenzy within seconds after closing a kid's bedroom door. Yes, indeed, we could teach street prostitutes a thing or two.

However, even when you're "in the mood," the odds are good that one of your children will wake up and wander into the bedroom at the most inopportune moment. I remember such a time when we were interrupted by my four-year-old daughter's voice: "What are you doing?" she asked incredulously as she stood at our door. My husband propelled himself off the bed and into his robe in seconds while I clutched the sheet to my neck. "Nothing!" we both shouted at the top of our lungs. I think our response frightened her more than anything she actually saw.

Some Encouraging Statistics

Marital bliss with children doesn't always seem possible, but the good news is that despite the stress and the arguments and the fatigue, recent studies show that almost all couples say that if they had it to do all over again, they would.

Redbook magazine's 1994 national survey looked at one thousand recent parents and found that nine out of ten couples said that, despite the rigors of child raising, they would do it all over again, and that they were happy they had had children. Here's some of the survey's additional findings:

- Sixty-four percent of fathers and 64 percent of mothers say the reality of family life is better than they imagined.
- Fifty-four percent of fathers and 56 percent of mothers say they became closer after they had children.
- Despite the energy drain kids place on a couple, two out of three men and women feel they get enough emotional attention from their spouse.

⇥ TIPS FROM THE TRENCHES ⇤

⟡ The only way my husband and I can have any real romance is when we drop off our kids at his parents' house and then return back to our house. There's something about an empty house that turns us both on! —*Cynthia, Saddle River, New Jersey*

❧ Not every time in bed has to end with the Big Orgasm. When my husband just lies with me on the couch after the kids go to sleep and sort of "pets" me without any pressure for it to end in actual intercourse, it make me much more willing to fool around.

—*Greta, St. Paul, Minnesota*

❧ I had to learn all over again how to flirt with my wife. After our second was born, and things were pretty grim in the sex department, I tried to remember how we had acted when we'd just met—I started using some of the old phrases and secret code words we had used. It got us back to those old feelings again.

—*Scott, Murfreesboro, Tennessee*

3

Preparing Your Child

Maggie, age three, upon being told that there's a new baby brother growing in her mother's tummy: "Can you give it back and get a girl baby?"

Sam, age four, after having repeatedly asked for a sibling and finally being told there would be a new baby in a few months: "I changed my mind. Never mind."

Tara, age five: "Can I being him to school with me for Show and Tell? . . . I'll be careful."

The biggest change in your child's life up to this point will undoubtedly be the addition of a sibling. Up until now he or she has been king of the hill, star of the show, the main attraction, the Only Child. What will happen when a new baby enters the picture? Will this adversely affect your first child's relationship with you? With your husband? Will your older child feel pushed out, ignored? What can be done to cushion the blow?

A new sibling affects each child differently. Some are thrilled with the prospect of soon having a playmate; others feel threatened by the idea of someone stealing attention from Mom and Dad. While there are no hard and fast rules, we do know that the older your child is—that is, the longer he or she has been the only child—the more effect this new sibling will have on your child as a whole. I certainly can attest to that.

Confessions of a Firstborn

When my sister was born, I was six and a half years old. Up until then life had been very pleasant for me. I had been the center of attention in my own family as well as the first grandchild on both sides of my extended family, so I was definitely sitting in the cat-bird seat: no competition from any direction. I had never given any thought to the concept of a sibling. My best friend next door was also an only child. As a result, I had no clue what an infant even looked like. When my mother became pregnant, she and my father sat me down and gave me the news, but it never really hit home. I knew my mother was "getting a baby," but I somehow pic-tured the baby as some kind of doll-like creature that was being brought into the world *for my own pleasure*—as another kind of present, in a long line of lovely presents. (It seemed wherever I went in those days I got presents.)

So it came as quite a shock the day my parents brought my sis-ter home from the hospital a week after she was born. I remember coming home from first grade (in those days you could walk home from school without an adult!) and finding my relatives sitting in the living room. That was nothing new; my grandparents and aunts often dropped by in the afternoon. But something was wrong—very wrong—with this picture. When I walked into the living room, for example, conversation did *not* halt. No one jumped up to give me a big hug and kiss. Not one person com-mented on my adorableness or my cute little outfit or my pretty blonde hair done up in braids. More important—to me—was the fact that my grandmother didn't exclaim, as she always did, "Here's our Joanie!" That had always been her greeting to me, and I loved it. The announcement never failed to stop conversation and focus all eyes on me as I made my various entrances; it made me feel like a kind of princess.

Not only did she not say it this time, she didn't even look up! In fact, no one looked up. Everyone seemed hunched over, leaning toward my aunt Rita, who was holding the Other One, as I came to call my newborn sister. Murmur, murmur, murmur, I heard from the group. "So sweet . . . so tiny . . . ," they cooed. It was sickening.

Then I heard my grandmother say, "Those are the bluest eyes I've ever seen." What? Could I have heard correctly? Traitor! *I* had the bluest eyes she'd ever seen! At least that's what she used to say to me. Unable to stand it anymore, I wandered into the kitchen where my mom was preparing a tray of cake and coffee. She did hug me hello as usual, but I could tell she was distracted. "Wash your hands, Joanie, if you want some cake," she said, and then left me standing there when the Other One started to cry.

From then on things went downhill. I had lost my crown to an interloper, and things were never the same. Throughout my childhood, however, I still managed to steal most of the attention from others through sheer grit on my part—I was in every school musical, singing and dancing up a storm; my piano pieces in recitals were the loudest, if not the best; and at family gatherings I completely controlled the actions of my sister and my cousins, who came along soon after my sister's arrival.

"Thank God, things were never the same," my mother says now. "Without a sibling you would have become a spoiled, impossible, self-absorbed child."

Whatever can she mean?

A Sibling Makes for Good Family Life

Like my mother, many parents look back on their two children and agree that not only did their first child "need" a sibling, but the parents "needed" another child to take their own intense focus off the first. Another child to grow and mature at his or her own rate, without unnecessary—and sometimes destructive—parental interference.

Despite the fact that some children do feel, as I did, that their world is invaded with the birth of a new baby, there are many other children who look forward to a new sibling with excitement and joy. Robert Steward, in *The Second Child*, found in his two-year longitudinal study of forty-one families that every single first-born reported that they *wanted* a sibling.

Dr. Elizabeth Ellis agrees with that finding. She finds jealousy over a new sibling is not as common as sometimes thought. "I think it's an overrated phenomenon. I see that most children are really thrilled about having a sibling. It may be that nature programs them to look forward to a sister or brother." She adds that unfortunately very young children have no idea that it will be quite a while before they can actually have the baby as a playmate. They don't realize that the baby's going to demand a great deal of attention and care from both Mom and Dad. "That's when it gets hard on the firstborn. The custodial care of a newborn is just all-consuming. It's hard for a preschooler to understand that the baby has to be fed every couple of hours, or that Mommy has to rock the baby a long time before it will go to sleep. Even adults forget the amount of time and energy a newborn takes. It makes for quite an adjustment for the older child."

Even if the oldest temporarily regresses back to thumb sucking or wetting the bed after the arrival of the baby—which is very common—in the end the child may mature more quickly. Studies reveal that kids show signs of more grown-up behavior—such as more independent feeding or toilet behavior—after the birth of the new baby, even if signs of regression are also there.

According to the American Academy of Pediatrics (AAP), almost 80 percent of us grow up with a least one brother or sister. And even if we don't get along with each other all the time, siblings can come to prove very positive roles in our lives. That's where we take our first steps toward learning about companionship, solving conflicts, negotiation techniques, and friendship. Siblings protect each other from the outside world and often stand united against parental demands.

Naturally, we all want to make the experience of another baby a positive one for our older child so that the whole sibling experience begins on a smooth path. We also want our older child adjusted to this idea before we bring home the new baby. As experienced moms, we know a newborn's needs are all-consuming. Most expectant mothers experience anxiety over this issue— mainly because they can't quite picture how they're going to handle two during those first few weeks. They also want their two kids to "be friends" and feel that by preparing their firstborn now, it will encourage that friendship down the road. But there is no proof that any kind of preparation of the older child has any lasting effect on sibling relationships. It may affect the child's initial reaction to the new baby, but that reaction can and does change a hundred times in the first month. It takes a long time for brothers and sisters to adjust to each other, and that relationship is an ongoing process continuing into adulthood.

However, preparing your child for a sibling can make the child's life easier once the new baby arrives. He or she will be able to accept this big upheaval much sooner knowing what to expect. The better prepared the child is, the smoother the transition will be for your firstborn—and for you.

Breaking the News

If your child is old enough to understand the abstract concept of another baby, you're probably faced with an even bigger challenge. How do you explain the very idea of a sibling? My own daughter was only eleven months old when I got pregnant again, so there was very little I could do to prepare her for the arrival of Alex. My friend Cheryl, however, was especially concerned about telling her son Patrick, who was just over three, when she became pregnant. "He was just old enough to understand what having a brother or sister meant and just young enough to not understand the ramifications of what caring for a newborn meant."

Cheryl, like most mothers, needed to consider not only when to tell her child, but how to tell him. All sorts of questions came up: How specific should she be? What details should she include? How a child reacts to the news of a new baby depends largely on his or her age at the time the baby is born. Knowing what to expect from each age group will make it easier to handle the adjustments needed in the months ahead.

Under Age Two

Most experts agree that if your child is under two years old, there is really not much to tell. You may be able to convey the vague idea that there is a baby growing in Mommy's tummy, but only in very general terms. When my daughter, at eighteen months, was introduced to her brother, she simply raised her eyebrows and slapped him on his head to say hello. Toddlers will usually greet the new baby with some kind of physical reflex, but will be unable to understand that the "thing" in the cradle is actually their brother or sister. Instead of trying to prepare a toddler, concentrate on spending extra time with the child during your pregnancy. If your toddler continues to question the process, say, "When mommies and daddies love each other, they make a baby. That's how you were born."

Ages Three to Five

"We were so excited about being pregnant again," says Jillian, "that we told our four-year-old after the fifth month. I was starting to show already, and we had told our parents and a few close friends." Her husband, Joe, recalls sitting together with Betsy. "We were kind of nervous, and I think Betsy sort of picked up on that because she sat really straight up and kept looking back and forth at us." They finally said, "Remember when your cousin Linda got a new brother last year? Well, you're going to have a new brother or sister too!" Jillian recalls that Betsy was very happy and excited and wanted to know when this was all going to happen. "I told her in about four months and her face just fell. That's a long time for a four-year-old. As the months wore on, she became so impatient. By then we realized we'd probably given her the news too soon."

It's a hard decision to make. Experts say wait awhile to tell your child, but don't wait too long. You don't want your child to find out from someone else or to overhear adults discussing the pregnancy. At this age, the best way to figure out a good time is to know your own child's sense of time and his or her level of patience. To give the child a more concrete sense of time, it helps to connect the due date with a nearby holiday or season. "He should be here in time for your birthday," or "She'll be celebrating Christmas with us" is easier to understand than a specific day and month, which, by the way, is not guaranteed anyway.

As far as how much to tell your child, the best advice is to keep it simple. Most kids aren't ready for the gory details of the conception, pregnancy, and childbirth at this age. "A new brother or sister is going to be born in July" is fine for starters. Then wait. Show by your tone of voice and your undivided attention that you welcome questions or comments. Does the child digest that piece of news? Does he or she ask further questions? Your child might want to know if he or she grew in your stomach the same way. Or a child may want to know how the new baby will be born. A child may jump right into the all-important question: "When will the baby be able to play video games with me?" If you know the sex of the baby and plan to let others know, then you can include that piece of information. The key is to follow your child's lead. Kids tend to ask only the questions they can handle at this point in their maturity level.

School-Age Children

Obviously, the older your child is the more you can tell him or her. A child may pick up on the vibes long before you were planning to talk about it. A seven- or eight-year-old, for example, understands the concept of time as well as biology and can be told much earlier.

"It was really important for us to be honest with Craig right from the get-go," Brenda says about her seven-year-old. "I knew I wouldn't be able to keep my pregnancy a secret for long, and I just didn't want him to hear about it on the playground at school, where I work as a teacher's aide. So we told him at about twelve weeks—right after we got the results from my amniocentesis." Brenda recalled that at age ten she had heard about her mother's pregnancy from the owner of the neighborhood deli! "I remember being so hurt that my mother hadn't told me before she told people outside the family. I guess that's why I made sure we told our son before we told anyone else—even my mother and father were told after Craig."

In his book *On Becoming a Family*, T. Berry Brazelton, M.D., advises parents to tell their child sooner rather than later, since an older child will sense a change in the family anyway, and it is less "artificial" to simply give the reason. In addition, Dr. Brazelton feels that when parents have a hard time telling their older children, it "stems from their reluctance to give up the previous relationship with the older child and the fear that they will not be able to make it with two children. The sooner parents accept the reality of the new baby, the sooner the child can. Then the mother can be freer to think about and relate to her fetus." He cautions that too much fussing and obsessing over the upcoming birth can be counterproductive. The key is to fit this news into the family structure so it becomes a natural process of family development.

The older your child is, the more questions he or she is likely to ask. These questions may come out of left field, and it's hard to anticipate them. The questions may center on Mom's well-being or the future sleeping arrangements. A child may react with happy excitement ("Oooh, finally—I hope it's a boy," or "I hope it's a girl") or with sullen rage ("We don't need anyone else") or with sadness. Listen carefully to your child's comments and, again, follow his or her lead. On the other hand, don't be surprised if there is little curiosity or interest in this pregnancy. Kids are pretty self-involved at this age; and although this is big news in your book, it may not be quite as important right now as tonight's episode of *Rug Rats*. Be prepared, however, for renewed interest at a later date. My daughter always saved her questions for the second before I turned out her bedroom light at night, when I was the least able to concentrate on anything due to that incredible evening fatigue many moms get.

You may want to use this pregnancy as an opportunity to talk about sexuality as a part of family life. This is a way to show your son or daughter the sacred connection between sharing love and creating a new life. Look for books in your local library with simple illustrations to show conception and pregnancy designed specifically for elementary schoolchildren. That way you can combine the big news with a bit of sex education at the same time. Be as honest as you can in this area. Use the correct anatomical word—"penis" instead of "wee wee gun," "vagina" instead of "pee pee place." It isn't, of course, necessary to describe in great detail what the placenta looks like or how the episiotomy is performed; we don't want to scare them witless, we just want to give them an idea of how their sister or brother will be born. Older children may ask more difficult questions, including personal inquiries into your own sex life. Know that you can set boundaries. For example, saying, "That's private between Daddy and me, just like it will be for you and your husband some day," lets them know some areas are off-limits.

Once you've broken the news, you may experience a sense of relief. Now you can concentrate on preparing your child for the arrival of the new baby. Many of the following ideas will depend on your child's age, but the general theme of each technique can work for all ages.

Tips on Preparing Your Child

Get Out the Baby Album

In our family, we are all big on taking lots of photos. As a result, we have lots of photo albums lining our bookshelves, and each child now has his or her own "baby book," which holds snapshots taken from the day of their birth through about age five. At the time Alex was due, however, I had only one baby book, with about one million shots of Annie, who was not even two years old at the time. But even that young, she loved to sit on my lap and go through the book, pointing at pictures of herself.

Showing youngsters pictures of themselves as babies is a good way to start to prepare them for the upcoming months. Pictures of being bathed in a tiny tub, getting their diapers changed, sleeping in a cradle or a crib, of a christening or bris celebration—all bring together the concept of what having a baby entails. Your child may ask, "Why was I crying in this picture?" and you can respond by saying that babies cry an awful lot, especially at first, but that crying is a new baby's only way of communicating. Young children are often very upset to hear a newborn's cries—sometimes they even blame themselves!—and knowing ahead of time that crying is the norm will ease their minds a bit.

Don't be afraid of sharing memories of the hard work that accompanies the joys of having a baby. "Yes, that picture of you in the car seat is cute, but Mommy sometimes had a hard time lifting it." Or, "See this picture of you in the high chair with chocolate pudding all over you? Babies spill lots of food on themselves, and that means parents have a lot of laundry to do." From there it's an easy leap into: "Mommies get very very busy with brand-new babies because babies need so much care." Try to keep these comments light and simple, so your child doesn't get a negative spin on the upcoming arrival. But it's important to prepare a child for the fact that once the baby is born you will not be able to give the child the kind of attention he or she has come to expect.

While going through the album, you may want to ask what things the child would like to teach the new baby. A child may offer to teach the baby to skateboard or to ride a two-wheeler, but at least he or she will have a solid sense of being a needed member of the family. You might ask in what ways your child could help you when you bring home the new baby. The child may suggest feeding or diapering the baby. My friend's daughter offered a spanking to make the baby stop crying! My friend laughed and suggested that maybe she could hold the baby instead, and that might keep the baby from crying, since new babies can never be spanked. Whatever your child suggests, try to run with it; your child's feedback helps you to better understand his or her feelings at this time.

Showing children pictures of themselves will also reassure them—at a time when they need extra reassurance—that they are very special. Look at all the photos Mom and Dad took! Look at Grandma and Grandpa pushing him in the swing! Look at the special baby outfit Aunt Mary knitted for her! You might remind your child, "You were the first baby in our family, and that will always make you very special." The concrete evidence of the photos serves to remind children of all the love that surrounds them.

Spend Time Together with a Baby

"It wasn't until I brought our five-year-old son, Ryan, to my neighbor's house and let him hold her four-month-old that he really started to get it. Until then he showed no interest whatsoever; I was beginning to worry that he was in denial about the whole thing. But after that visit, he started to ask questions about feeding and diapering newborns," says one mother. "The idea of 'baby' finally became a reality to him."

If it's true that a picture is worth a thousand words, then seeing the real thing is worth a thousand pictures. You might even volunteer to do some baby-sitting for a new mother. That way your child can see you doing many of the same chores you'll be doing with your own infant very soon. Let your child help with some of the work. A child can unfold the diaper or hold the bottle or shake the rattle. This is a good time to introduce the idea that he or she will be helping you and your husband out when the new baby arrives and that you will not be able to spend so much time with him or her—at least for the first few weeks. Add that at that time he or she will be acquiring special privileges too. Mention that he might be able to stay up a half hour later now that he's a big brother. Or that she can ride her bike down to the corner or have two playmates come over at the same time once the new baby arrives. This gives the child something else to look forward to.

Baby-sitting will also give you an opportunity to hone your mothering skills. It is really amazing how much we forget—or block out!—about caring for a newborn. You may get some new pointers on caring for a baby too. There may have been new gadgets and technology invented since the birth of your child; I was amazed at the pink-and-blue disposable diapers and the new high-tech baby monitors that came out when my son was born.

If baby-sitting someone else's baby isn't feasible, look for an opportunity for you and your child to spend some time with a newborn and its mother. Take your child with you when you drop off a baby gift at your neighbor's, for example.

If you are planning on breast-feeding, it would be a good idea to let your child witness a mother nursing her baby so that your child won't be too shocked seeing you doing it in the near future. If the nursing mother doesn't mind having wide eyes staring close range at her nipples, she might answer some questions from your curious child.

If there are no handy infants around, you could consider visiting your local hospital. Most maternity wards welcome young visitors, depending on age; call ahead to find out visiting hours and possible restrictions. You might even get lucky and see a baby close up. In my local hospital, for example, kids can watch nurses bottle-feed some infants in the maternity ward. And don't forget about your pediatrician's office, where babies are everywhere. Most moms are quite happy to show off their new babies to other children. Warn your child ahead of time not to touch the baby without the mom's permission.

Make Any Big Changes Before the Baby Comes

Ideally, the less developmental adjustment your child has to go through before there's a newborn in the house, the better. Since so much of the family's life will be in a state of upheaval in the beginning, it is best if your child's life remains constant. This will give the child a sense of security. But it often works out that around the time a mother gets pregnant, her child is going through important transitions. A toddler will most likely be involved in potty training or getting ready for her "big girl" bed. Dr. Pinsoff suggests that if possible these changes should be made well in advance of the sibling's birth. "If it looks like the transition may spill into the time the new baby arrives, then wait until at least a month after the birth," he advises. The worst scenario seems to be trying to imitate or continue the change during the baby's homecoming period. Also, it is common for firstborns to regress into old habits for a little while, so even if a toddler has become potty trained, it is likely he or she will have a few "accidents" for a while.

If your child goes to preschool or has regularly scheduled day care, continue in the same routine throughout the pregnancy and after your second born has arrived. The less upset to the child's routine, the better, especially to very young children.

Some mothers feel so guilty about having a second child that they take their firstborn out of day care while they're pregnant. "I just thought my daughter and I needed quality time before the new baby, so I took off a few days of work and took her out of kindergarten," states Rowanda, an insurance adjuster. "It was a big mistake. She missed her friends and actually got kind of anxious because her routine was interrupted, and all I did was clean the kitchen cabinets." Looking back, Rowanda thinks it would have been better to spend more time after school. "Taking her to the park or to get an ice cream would have seemed like a bigger treat," she says now.

Get the House Ready Together

The idea behind involving your firstborn in the house preparation is to minimize any adjustment the child will have to make as well as to make him or her feel like a part of the festivities. A child should feel like he or she is getting ready to welcome a sibling into the family. The most important consideration to decide is where the new baby will sleep—at least for the first few weeks. Make the sleeping arrangements as far in advance as possible during your pregnancy. The ideal situation is to put your newborn in a separate room from your firstborn. That way your child has less of an adjustment to make. Even toddlers view their room as a sanctuary. If your child has a bed as well as a crib because he or she is still in transition, leave it as it is. As impractical as it sounds, it worked out better for us to borrow a cradle and put it in the nursery rather than move Annie's crib into that room. Despite the fact that she had pretty much moved into her "big girl" bed, she still had territorial rights to the crib for quite a while. It became a sort of security blanket for her, particularly during her brother's first few months at home. Luckily, by the time Alex had outgrown the cradle, she had gotten over her possessiveness of her crib, and we were able to return the cradle and move the crib into Alex's room.

If two bedrooms are impossible, then try to provide a separate space for your firstborn's toys and books. Include the child in this. Ask where he or she would like the crib, for example. Be solicitous of the child's preferences. Don't divide the room in half right away; after all, your newborn won't know about space issues for a while. You may know ahead of time that you will want the crib or cradle in your bedroom for the first few weeks. Mothers who nurse their firstborn often decide to keep their new baby next to them in a cradle in order to facilitate breast-feeding. "I knew after my first that it was just a waste of time to go into the nursery every hour, nurse, then go back. It was easier to plan of having my second in the same room with me," states one nursing mother. In that case let your first child know he or she won't be sharing a room for a while.

Most firstborns like feeling included in the practical preparations for the new baby. You might ask the child's opinion on where to place the changing table, for example. Show an older child, if the child's interested, how to wind up the baby swing and turn on the baby monitor. This is an opportunity to role play, to have pretend games, and to make the chores into playtime. One mother played "baby" and cried into the baby monitor while her three-year-old played mommy. When we bought a double stroller in preparation for my son's birth, Annie put her favorite doll in the other seat; when we went on walks she talked to the baby, showing him around the neighborhood. Unfortunately, it came as a great disappointment that when Alex did join us, he was asleep most of the time. Get out your child's baby clothes and ask—don't tell—if he or she wouldn't mind if the new baby "borrowed" them for a while. You might have the child select an outfit for the baby to wear home from the hospital. If you've saved your child's baby toys, ask the child to choose a "welcome" toy to place in the crib. Ask your child to make some special drawings to put on the wall near the changing table or the crib.

One caveat to keep in mind. There is a good chance that your child will not be interested in this upcoming event. Some mothers report that their child knew what was going on, but it never became that big a deal. For some kids, the time sequence is too complicated; for others, house duties aren't a big priority. If that's the case, back off. Don't force a child to join you in the preparations. When kids, especially older ones, feel that a certain idea is being crammed down their throats, they tend to shut off.

"I wanted to sit down and read books on procreation together—it was my great fantasy that my nine-year-old and I would pick out wallpaper for the baby's room, choose a mobile, and hang up baby clothes on those little hangers together," recalls Amanda. "Well, she couldn't be bothered. She was going into middle school that fall, and she was more concerned about cheerleading tryouts. When she started rolling her eyes at my mention of diaper ointment, I knew I had to back off."

With older kids, especially, too much preparation may turn off their enthusiasm. Adolescents, for example, may refuse to be read to but may pick up magazines and books scattered casually in the family room. That is, when no one is looking. So be prepared to accept your child's reluctance as well as his or her enthusiasm in getting your home ready for the new arrival.

Have Your Child Spend Time with Daddy and Other Caregivers

One father, interviewed by Stewart (*The Second Child*) on parenting two children, said it best: "It took one child to make my wife a mother; it took two children to make me a father." It is during a second pregnancy that Dad usually gets closer to his child. One reason may be that Mom is so busy with the newborn that she eases up on her attention to the firstborn, allowing Dad to get closer. Mom may also be too worn out to continue with her prior level of child involvement.

Regardless of the reason, it's important to encourage your husband to make a concerted effort to increase his child care activities with your child while you are still pregnant. After all, in a few months he will be home alone for a couple of days with his firstborn. He will *have* to put forth more effort then. Studies show that fathers spend more time sharing household chores and parenting duties when the second child arrives. But don't wait until the new baby is born. Start beforehand to establish a routine. This is an opportunity for father and child to have special time together. Here's what some fathers did with their sons and daughters while their wives were pregnant:

+ Took his son to his yearly checkup.
+ Washed the car together.
+ When on a shopping spree with his daughter and bought diapers, ointment, baby thermometer, a new mattress for the crib, and new room-darkening shades for the nursery.
+ Listened to a home "recital" after his son's clarinet lesson.
+ Camped out with his son in the backyard (until 9:00 P.M.).
+ Went to his daughter's parent conference.
+ Checked math homework with his third grader.

Involve other caretakers, too, in spending more time with your firstborn before the big event. Grandmothers and grandfathers can become part of a routine in caretaking duties now, so your child becomes used to their involvement.

If you plan on hiring child care help once the baby is born, have the person come over periodically during the latter part of your pregnancy to become acquainted with your child. Besides, you could use the time alone once a week or so during the third trimester—even if your time alone means sneaking upstairs and putting your feet up for an hour! Use the time to "practice" taking care of yourself once the baby comes.

Sign Up for Sibling Preparation Classes

Despite the preparation you've given your firstborn, you may want to enroll the child in a class that teaches him or her about the birthing process in language the child can understand. Hospitals throughout the country—especially university teaching hospitals—have begun offering sibling preparation classes for the soon-to-be big sisters and brothers. These classes are designed to help foster the child's positive self-image while offering guidance to assist overall family adjustment. Most sibling preparation classes focus on helping children cope with their concerns about the birth, the hospital setting, and their feelings about the new baby.

At St. Paul Medical Center in Dallas, educators Maria Montes and Maxine Adcox, R.N., teach an hour-and-a-half sibling preparation class for children aged two to ten years old. "Our classes begin in the conference room where the children sit in a semi-circle with their parents, and we discuss their feelings about hearing that they'll be having a brother or sister. We then go into the story of pregnancy and childbirth—including both vaginal and cesarean births—using two 'pregnant' rag dolls," explains Montes. One doll has a separate knitted "uterus" and a tiny "baby" connected by a yarn "umbilical cord" and cloth "placenta"; this baby come out vaginally. The other doll has a slit in her stomach and the baby comes out as a cesarean. "Are the kids squeamish at watching this demonstration?"

"Not at all," insists Montes. "To the contrary, the children are fascinated with the process, and often ask their mothers how, exactly, *they* were born." After discussing bottle-feeding and breast-feeding, the class takes a tour of a labor, delivery, and recovery room—otherwise known as birthing room—and the postpartum area. Here they may meet a new mother who will allow them to see—not touch—her newborn. "The kids look at the umbilical cord and say hello to the mom. There are a lot of ooh's and ah's from this crowd," continues Montes. The class then returns to the conference room to view a short video called *I'm a Little Bit Jealous*, told from the point of view of an older sister after the birth of her brother. The class concludes with some hands-on lessons on diapering and holding a baby. Children leave with a Big Brother/Sister Button and certificate. The cost per child is ten dollars.

Some hospitals may not have formal classes but many have sibling tours available. The Highland Park Hospital in Highland Park, Illinois, for example, uses trained volunteers in their birthing center to give a private forty-five-minute tour to the "expectant" sibling and her parents. The tour includes a look at the nursery and the birthing room where the mom will be for two or three days, as well as a trip to the juice machine and snack area reserved for siblings. In the lounge area the child is given a "newborn" doll to hold and feed, and picture books showing the pregnancy and childbirth process.

To locate sibling preparation classes and tours, call your local hospital, childbirth educator, midwife, or OB-GYN.

Special Circumstances

Today families come in all different shapes and packages, with half siblings, stepsiblings, and children who come into the family through adoption.

Stepfamilies

Countless American children are faced with the divorce of their parents and often their subsequent remarriage to others. And when Mom or Dad is expecting a new baby with a stepparent, that adjustment is often even tougher. "I think my son held on to some secret wish that somehow my husband and I would get back together—even after I remarried," remarks Meg. "But when I became pregnant again, he had to face the reality that that would never happen."

In addition to the natural jealousy firstborns feel about the arrival of the new baby, half siblings may also feel resentment that their parent is starting a new family or that the new baby gets to live with a "real" mother and father. According to the American Academy of Pediatrics, the older the stepchild is, the less threatened the child will be by a new half sibling. However, resentments are likely to surface in all firstborns because of the attention the infant will receive. The AAP suggests that the birth parent be as truthful as possible about what is to happen and be diligent about making the child feel a part of the preparation. In addition, be sure to spend extra private time together each day to make your firstborn feel like he or she is the most important person in your life. Allow children to voice their feelings concerning the arrival of a half sibling.

Many families say that talking with other stepfamilies can be helpful. "Thank God Brianna became friends with the new girl in the third-grade class—who was part of a stepfamily—at around the same time I was pregnant," recalls Catherine. "Brianna became more accepting of having a half sibling, I think, because her new friend has experienced the same thing."

Despite these challenges firstborns face, the AAP reports that half siblings tend to become good friends and companions, and in time their relationships are rewarding.

Adoption

Years ago, parents were turned down if they sought to adopt a child after having had a child by birth. Child experts believed that the two children shouldn't be mixed; they'd be too different in background and personality. But today, adoption agencies place children with families who already have biological children. A study published by *The Journal of Genetic Psychology* found that placement of a child in an adoptive family does not affect overall adjustment of a couple's biological child. In fact, the study found positive effects on the adopted child in much the same way biological children experience benefits from siblings.

There may be any number of reasons why parents may consider adopting. Secondary infertility is one of the most common. Still, adoptive families will need to pay special attention to the needs of each of their children. The National Adoption Information Clearinghouse in Washington, D.C., offers some tips for parents with adoptive families:

Preparing an Adopted Child for a Birth Sibling: Be very sensitive to your adopted child's fear that you may love your birth child more. Acknowledge the differences there will be between each. Stress that though each sibling joins the family in a different way, that you'll treasure them both.

Preparing a Birth Child for an Adopted Sibling: Realize that your birth child will question the need for this adoption. Be as honest as you can, sending the message that this sibling will be an equal part of the family. Stress that first children are special, whether they are a birth child or adopted, and that the second child is special too.

Share the adoption process with your child. There will probably be paperwork, possibly a trip to a foreign country, a visit from a social worker and/or the birth parents. The more your first child is involved, the more likely he or she will be excited about the new family member.

⇥ TIPS FROM THE TRENCHES ⇤

❖ While my wife was pregnant, the cat on our farm was also expecting. We let our daughter watch the birth of the kittens in the barn. She was really thrilled, and I think it helped her understand more about childbirth. She kept one of the kittens as her own pet, and that sort of distracted her from her jealousy over her new sibling.   —*John, Franksville, Wisconsin*

◆ Be careful what you say in front of your preschooler during your pregnancy. My son, Christopher, overheard me complaining to my girlfriends about having hemorrhoids. By the next day, his entire kindergarten class knew I had hemorrhoids. According to his teacher, he had stood up and made a general announcement right after the Pledge of Allegiance. The kids didn't know what hemorrhoids were, exactly, but they knew I had them!

—*Kathy, East Northport, New York*

◆ My kids were just thirteen months apart, so I knew I'd better be organized. While I was expecting my second, I approached the whole custodial duties in terms of a time line. I tried to prepare each child—and myself—for the next phase of development. I was ready when my oldest was potty training while my youngest was teething. I jotted down each state in a journal so I could pretty much predict when the next child would reach that stage."

—*Carol, Lilburn, Georgia*

 **II**

Childbirth . . . the Second Time Around

4
The Labor

My water broke in the bathroom, in the middle of potty training my daughter. I was trying to get her to sit on the potty; I squatted next to her and suddenly there was a pool of water. My daughter pointed and shrieked, "Mommy went wee-wee!"   —*Flossie, Madison, Wisconsin*

Mine broke while my husband was at work. The first person I called was our baby-sitter. *Then* I remembered to call my husband!   —*Louise, San Diego, California*

Mine broke at my daughter's Brownie meeting, where I was Cookie Mom, handing out boxes of peanut butter patties on the patio. All eight girls stared in horror as the water gushed out onto the driveway. My daughter was really embarrassed. So much for female bonding!
                    —*Suze, Rapid City, South Dakota*

The odds are good that when the time comes to have your second baby, your first child will probably be nearby to watch the preliminary drama unfold. If you are alone with your child at the onset of your labor, which is often the case with a second pregnancy, it can be quite disconcerting to have to deal with your youngster's needs at the same time you're timing contractions and trying to remember how to breathe.

"My contractions were coming seven minutes apart," remembers Katie. "I had called my husband at work and my mother was on her way, but there I was with my daughter, braiding her American Girl doll's hair while I was doing the Lamaze breathing! I just didn't want her to get scared."

Mothers agree that going into labor with their second baby is a completely different experience from their first. "The first time I was only concerned with myself. I was very afraid of the pain, and I couldn't get past that. With my second, I was consumed with details: "Would the baby-sitter get here on time? Would my son start to cry if he saw me in pain?"

Michelle felt much more in control with her second labor: "With my first baby, I raced to the hospital the minute I had my first contraction. I think I figured that the hospital would somehow make the labor go away! The second time I wasn't in such a hurry to get there. I knew from experience I'd just be in some room waiting. Instead, I did most of the waiting at home with my family."

Her sister, Alexis, was driving on the expressway with her son when she felt her first contraction. "I pretended everything was just fine, but every time I took a superloud cleansing breath he looked really strangely at me. He knew something was up, but I didn't know what to say to him that wouldn't frighten him. I knew I couldn't deal with his crying *and* me in labor, so I just tried to hide it from him."

Should You Hide Your Labor
from Your Child?

Not necessarily, says Marion McCartney of the American College of Nurse-Midwives. "Historically in our society there's been so much fear and mystery surrounding labor and birth that our kids grow up being confused and apprehensive about the whole subject. It's usually better to be honest and open with your children." McCartney cautions, however, that your degree of openness should depend on the age of your child. "Two- or three-year-olds are easily frightened, especially if they see you are in pain. They haven't really separated from you yet at that age—they think they're still a part of you—so when they see you suffering, they hurt too."

McCartney suggests that mothers use their own judgment with older children. "You know what upsets your child and what doesn't," she says. "But kids can handle more than you think." For mothers of four- and five-year-olds, McCartney suggests simple explanations in easy-to-understand language, sprinkled with assurance that Mommy will be okay. Here are some examples:

- "A contraction is like a bump in my tummy. It hurts a little, but that's the way the baby gets born.
- "It means the baby is coming down my stomach—soon the contractions will come faster and faster, and then your sister or brother will come out!"
- "There's a special way Mommy can breathe when the contraction comes so that it doesn't hurt so much."
- "After a contraction Mommy feels just fine. She just has to rest to get ready for the next one."
- "Soon I'll go into a special room where the doctor/ midwife and nurses will help the baby be born."

Planning Ahead for the Trip

The best way to help your child during your initial labor is to have a plan for his or her care when it's time to go to the hospital. Who will you call? A member of the family is ideal, but if you have no family living nearby, you have to depend on friends, neighbors, or your baby-sitters. In my own case, I had two backup plans. Since neither my husband nor I had extended family living within one hundred miles, I knew we were at the mercy of our baby-sitters. There was no possibility of taking our daughter to the hospital with us; at the time she was only eighteen months old. Annie's beloved sitter Kate was a part-time student at a nearby college, and she insisted we call her "day or night" whenever I went into labor. "I can be there in less than a half an hour," she promised. Still, I couldn't depend on her to be sitting home by the phone during the entire month of April, so we agreed I'd call her mother, who lived around the corner, if she didn't answer the phone. In addition, my next-door neighbor offered to take Annie to her house in the event that Kate or her mother were unavailable. As kind as my neighbor was, I knew she would be my last choice because in that case Annie would have to stay with her and her children. I wanted to keep my daughter at home in her own environment where she could continue her daily routine as much as possible. Still, knowing I had several options really helped me to sleep better those last few weeks of my pregnancy. As it turned out, my water broke at 11:00 P.M. on a Sunday night, and Kate was at our house twenty minutes later. We never had to use the backups, but I was glad to have them there.

There's more to planning ahead than simply having a baby-sitter on call, however. Although, by now, your child is prepared for a brother or sister, your child may not be prepared for what happens to Mommy when the baby comes. Does your child know that mommy will be going to the hospital or birthing center? Does your child know that Aunt Mary will be staying while Daddy takes mommy to the hospital? Does your child understand it may take a very long time before he or she can see the baby? Remember, a toddler or preschooler's sense of time can be quite distorted. Three hours can seem like a whole day, and twelve hours is an eternity. Since you really won't know for sure how long your labor will be—unless you have a preplanned cesarean—you will need to prepare your child for the seemingly endless wait. Saying, "You might have to wait until after school before the baby comes," or "Aunt Mary might stay overnight if the baby doesn't come right away," can give your child a more concrete understanding of time.

Mothers can plan for their absence in other ways that will make the separation from their first child less painful (see chapter 1). If you haven't taken your child to any sibling preparation classes at your hospital, then it may be worth a trip to the maternity ward, if possible, as well as to the gift shop and the cafeteria for a snack. Remind your child that you'll be phoning during the time you're there.

Should Your Child Accompany You to the Hospital?

Only if the child is old enough—and extremely patient and comfortable in hospitals. Most experts agree that children age seven and younger simply do not have the patience to sit through a labor in the waiting room. Even older children can become anxious at the sight of hospital equipment and the sounds of laboring moms. It's best to keep children at home. That is, unless you have been planning on a sibling-attended birth (see chapter 5).

What Makes This Labor Different

The best part about a second labor is that you've done it all before. The fact that you're now an experienced "laborer" will make this labor seem smoother and easier. The familiar surroundings of the hospital and the memory of your first labor and delivery—if it was a positive experience—will help keep panic at bay. I remember being wheeled into the labor room and seeing the same nurses who'd delivered my daughter there. We all laughed at the idea of my being back there so soon—less than eighteen months later—but in a strange way it felt a little like coming home.

There is a strong probability that this labor will be familiar to you, barring an emergency cesarean, breech birth, or other complication. But despite your experience, there are several distinct characteristics of a typical second labor:

The Onset of Labor May Not Be as Clear-cut

The old wives' tale that false labor happens more in a second pregnancy is generally true. You are more likely to feel the irregular Braxton-Hicks contractions before you actually go into labor. Many mothers report stronger and more frequent Braxton-Hicks contractions with a second pregnancy.

The Actual Labor Tends to Be Shorter

This is the best news of all. Although figures vary, childbirth experts agree that a second labor can take almost half as long as the first. An average first labor is about fourteen hours, while a second averages eight hours. According to Dr. Nancy Rose, OB-GYN and associate professor of obstetrics and reproductive genetics at University of Pennsylvania's Health Systems Medical Center, a woman dilates 1.2 centimeters an hour in an average first labor compared to 1.5 centimeters an hour in her second. Why is the second labor shorter? "The pelvic walls have already been stretched with the birth of your first baby so dilation occurs quicker," explains Dr. Rose. "The cervix is ripe and soft and labor becomes a smoother process, usually." In fact, she cautions women who have already had a relatively short first labor—under six hours—to be prepared to have the second baby even faster in order to avoid a "taxicab birth." One word of warning: There is always the chance that you may be one of the few who experience a longer or more difficult labor the second time around, so don't count on an easy-breezy labor as a given or you may be in for bitter disappointment.

If your first baby was delivered by cesarean section and this will be your first vaginally delivered birth, then you will be having, for all practical purposes, a "first labor"—that is, your labor will be as long and as varied as a typical first childbirth labor.

Contractions May Feel Stronger

This happens in labors that are significantly shorter than the first. The contractions seem stronger because the whole process has been speeded up. For example, my second labor lasted only a couple of hours—compared with six hours for my first—yet I had the feeling that I couldn't control these contractions or get ahold of the deep-breathing process at first. With my first child I had gone through the three stages of labor just like the books said, and I had used the different breathing techniques for each stage. With the first birth my contractions had started out very faint and widely spaced so that I was able to get used to the idea. This time I was in a panic because I thought I had forgotten how to do the breathing correctly. I remember complaining to the nurse that the breathing wasn't "working" as well this time. That was because I was already eight centimeters dilated by the time I got to the hospital. In less than an hour I gave birth!

Your Second Baby May Come Earlier than Your First

Dr. Rose states that while there's no clear-cut reason, a first baby tends to show up after the due date while a second baby tends to be early. Often a first baby may be from two days to a week overdue, and the second baby may be two days to a week early. In my case, my first was seven days late and my second was six days early.

You May Be Considered "High Risk" with This Labor and Have More Medical Intervention

If you are over thirty-five, you may have already had a prenatal test, such as an amniocentesis. However, Dr. Rose states that if you've had a history of miscarriages, or if you've developed diabetes or high blood pressure during this pregnancy, your labor may be more carefully monitored than your first one.

The Pushing Stage Is Shorter and Easier

"Because the cervix has already accommodated a baby, it will be more ready for your second," explains Dr. Rose. "Since the ease of passage through the birth canal is generally a smoother process with a second baby, you may be wheeled into the delivery room as soon as the cervix is dilated." In a first birth, most pushing is done in the labor room, and patients are not moved to the delivery room until the baby's head crowns. It's interesting to note, though, that many hospitals today provide an LDR (labor/delivery/recovery) room—in order to avoid moving the mother at all.

In general, this labor will seem easier because everything is familiar. Knowing what the birthing room or delivery room is like and what pain medication can do helps a great deal. Many mothers say they were able to focus on remembering the thrill of their first child's actual birth during the hardest stages of labor in their second.

How to Make This Labor Better

By now you've already prepared yourself for this birth in a different way. Maybe you've sought out a different childbirth provider or even a different hospital or birthing center. If you're staying with the same provider, you've probably discussed the basics of this second pregnancy and feel better prepared in general.

But there are ways to use your first labor to your advantage in order to make this labor easier on you. McCartney suggests the following tips to healthy, low-risk second-time mothers, based on her years as a nurse-midwife:

Review Your First Labor and Devise a Labor Plan

Often having experienced a difficult first childbirth, many mothers make sure they've gone over a birth plan with their doctor or provider this time around, covering such topics as a second episiotomy and cesarean versus VBAC (vaginal birth after a cesarean). McCartney stresses, however, that it's also necessary to lay out specifics for your labor ahead of time. Don't start telling your doctor what you want when you're already seven centimeters dilated. Think back over your first labor and try to remember what helped and what hindered your laboring process. Ask yourself the following questions:

- What do you wish you had known beforehand?
- Do you want to be able to walk around during labor? If so, then you can't be hooked up to a fetal monitor throughout the entire labor.
- Can you take a shower or lie in a tub—some birthing centers have now installed whirlpools—or will you be confined to a bed?
- How often do you want to be examined during your labor?
- Who will be allowed in the laboring room and the delivery room with you besides your coach?
- Will your pubic area be shaved as a routine hospital procedure, or can that be avoided?
- What can you drink during labor?

I remember being allowed only ice chips; today McCartney suggests Coca-Cola. "Labor's the only time I recommend soda; the sugar does give energy; the Coke settles the stomach."

The labor plan is not intended as a script, but as an expression of preference. Some possible examples of what to include in a labor plan:

- Would like to be able to walk around; possibly take shower.
- External fetal monitoring only as required by the condition of the baby.
- Prefer no enema.
- No shaving of pubic hair.
- Want to avoid medications as much as possible.
- Would like to have music playing.

Discuss Pain Management Beforehand

With your first baby, did you receive an epidural too soon and was your delivery adversely affected? Or was it too late, so that by the time it kicked in you had already delivered and were now numb from the waist down? What other medications worked? If you were given Demeral with your first labor, did it make you sleepy and keep you from pushing—thus slowing down your labor? Or was the dosage so minimally effective that you could have skipped it? Were there other methods of pain management that seemed to help the first time around? A back rub for back labor? Taking a walk outside? A certain position you discovered late in your first labor that you could use throughout this second one? Now that you're familiar with the pain of labor, you're far better equipped to judge what—if any—drugs you'll need. "Second-time laboring moms often need far less drugs; they can pace themselves. They are better at breathing through contractions. They know that if they have more control over the labor—that is, they can move around, take a shower, and so on—they are more comfortable. The more comfortable they are, the less panic they have and the more they can handle pain," says McCartney.

Stay Home and Labor As Long As Possible

One of the advantages of going through labor for the second time is that you are familiar with the various stages—and with your own body's responses to discomfort and pain. A pregnant mother can usually differentiate between "serious" labor and faint, manageable contractions. McCartney suggests that second-time mothers labor at home for as long as possible. "Once you're admitted into a hospital, you become 'the patient,' and you're really bound by their rules, not your own. So if you are experiencing mild contractions, try to go about your regular activities—or ask your husband to go on a walk with you around the block. (You may be taking your toddler along in his or her stroller!) I tell healthy, low-risk moms to wait until they're at least four centimeters dilated before they check into their birthing center or hospital." How do you know if you're four centimeters dilated when no one is examining you? McCartney responds: "You'll know because that's when labor begins to become 'serious.' You'll remember the sensation that things are getting a bit more intense." A variety of symptoms may include a "bloody show," a flushed face, longer, stronger, and more regular contractions—five to ten minutes apart.

Intermittent Fetal Monitoring Only

Many hospitals use an electronic fetal monitor as a routine procedure during the entire labor. If you experienced this during your first labor, you know that it's necessary for the mother to lie still on a bed or gurney while belts that monitor the baby's heartbeat are placed around her abdomen. This confinement, McCartney believes, begins a spiral of unnecessary medical intervention. "Constant fetal monitoring is not only unnecessary on healthy women, it can be a hindrance because doctors, nurses, and technicians often overinterpret what's on the monitor." She explains a typical scenario: "If an average, healthy laboring mother cannot move around, she becomes more and more uncomfortable. In her misery, her contractions seem worse because she can't really control them. Then she needs narcotics for the pain. The drugs tend to slow down labor or interfere with the fetal heartbeat. The fetal monitor says the baby's in distress, and then it's C-section time."

The American College of Nurse-Midwives has suggested a system of intermittent fetal monitoring that allows the average, healthy, laboring mother to be free to move around if she wants. The baby's heart can be monitored at certain points during the labor: monitor about every half hour in early labor, taking the belts off in between to allow the mother to move into different positions or to be free to walk around. As labor progresses, monitor every fifteen or twenty minutes in active labor and every five minutes or during every contraction closer to delivery. For more information, visit the ACNM web site at www.acnm.org.

Make a Plan with Your Labor Coach Ahead of Time

While you're thinking through your labor plan, remember to include a talk with your labor coach. If you have the same coach as last time, then you both have the advantage of being able to learn from your first laboring experience. More often than not, first coaching experiences are not particularly successful ones. I can personally attest to that.

When I was pregnant the first time, my husband had dutifully gone with me to our childbirth classes, but I could tell he was not engaged in much that the instructor was saying. I comforted myself with the notion that once I went into labor, he would come through. I had fantasies that he'd be right there, breathing with me, focusing with me, massaging my belly—you know, like the childbirth movie. The one we saw had a kind of gauze sheen to it, with New Age music playing in the background accompanied by some tasteful groaning by the laboring mom. A Perfect Husband knelt by her, wiping her brow and obviously knowing all the right moves. I came away from that movie thinking that the husband could actually make the pains go away! Naturally I was shocked—shocked—to find out during my labor that my husband was unable to make me feel any better at all. Instead, he made it worse.

"What's happening? Are you having a contraction? Is it bad? Does it hurt? Should I get the doctor?" He'd ask anxiously as I was trying to count my breaths. Then he'd pat my stomach and stroke my arm. I wanted to shoot him.

"Don't touch me!" I'd snarl at him in between pants.

But I'm happy to report that things went much better the second time around because we sat down before I went to the hospital and went over what I would want—or would probably want—from him during this labor. The interesting thing is that when I actually thought about it, what I wanted most was for him to be there next to me, supporting me. I didn't need him to breathe with me or to give me directives—just to serve as my protector, my comforter. But I knew from experience that he needed specifics, and I knew from experience what really bugged me during labor, so here's what I offered:

- Don't talk to me during a contraction because I need to concentrate on the breathing.
- Don't touch me during a contraction unless I reach for you. The exception is if I'm on a fetal monitor and you can see the contraction, follow it with me, saying something like, "It's just about to peak . . . it's peaking now . . . it's going down . . ." to encourage me. If I tell you to shut the hell up, then that's an indication to stop talking.
- Don't chat with the technicians or tell jokes to the nurses.
- Ignore my nasty disposition.
- Don't leaf through *Sports Illustrated.*
- Don't leave me even for a minute; I'll get scared.
- Have the Chapstick ready.
- If something goes wrong during the labor, tell me immediately.

As irrational as some of my requests were, I knew I had to communicate them to my husband; because we'd gone through all this before, we at least knew what to expect from one another. As a result, my second labor was a huge improvement. My husband says that just going through it once before gave him a much better sense of what to do. His advice: "Don't *do* anything. I realized the second time around I couldn't stop the pain. But just by being there I helped. Encourage her and support her, and don't get hurt when she curses you out."

A More Seasoned Coach

My story is much more common than not. Although some couples report reaching an incredible closeness during that first labor, many mothers report that they were disappointed in their husband's failure to help them. Fathers admitted to feeling clumsy and helpless. Most were startled at their wife's "bad mood" once she went into active labor.

"I made some mistakes the first time," admits Dave, the father of two girls. "I couldn't tell what she wanted. I tried to help her with contractions, but she seemed to want to do it alone. She just seemed so angry. In fact, at one point I went into her goody bag and ate one of her lemon drop candies. She actually hit me."

Another father reports, "After the childbirth classes I thought I could help my wife cope with the pain, but I wasn't prepared for the intensity of it. I felt really helpless."

Mike, the father of a two-year-old, is worried about his wife's upcoming second birth. "The first time around we were both prepared for natural childbirth," he says. "After fourteen hours of labor my wife ended up having a cesarean. It was a real letdown for both of us. This time we're hoping for a VBAC, but I'm afraid it'll turn into another C-section."

Tips for Second-Time Coaches

Brad Sachs, Ph.D., a family therapist and director of the Father Center in Columbia, Maryland, a program focused on the needs and concerns of new and expectant fathers, believes couples who had a disappointing first labor can work together to make the second labor more positive if they first acknowledge what went wrong the first time around. "A father can help his wife to accept and grieve for the disappointment of the first labor by talking through it," states Sachs. "Couples can learn that each spouse had his or her own disappointments. Maybe the mother was upset at what she perceived as his lack of involvement or inability to anticipate her needs. Maybe the father was disappointed that she didn't respond to his techniques, or perhaps he had secretly been hoping for a boy instead of a girl." The important thing that each must do before the second labor, advises Sachs, is to let go of his or her "fantasy" labor and childbirth so that they don't repeat the scenario the second time around, which will just continue the cycle of resentment/guilt/disappointment.

"If, in their discussion, a husband acknowledges feeling overwhelmed and bewildered at the first labor and clearly doesn't think he will be able to help much in the second labor, then it's important that he admits this," says Sachs. "Saying 'Don't count on me this time; let's get your sister or mother as a coach, or use a *doula* to help out,' allows the couple to move on. Not every father is able to be a good coach. He can provide support in other ways.

"If, on the other hand, the dad feels that this time he will be ready to be more involved, or simply wants to try again, then he should communicate that, too. 'Give me another chance,' he could say. 'This time I know how to be a better coach for you.'"

For the second labor, Sachs suggests that fathers talk about their responsibilities earlier in the pregnancy. Here are some of his additional suggestions for fathers:

◆ Attend to your other child to make sure your wife is free to attend to her labor. A mom will usually feel neglectful and guilty about leaving her child—even to have another baby. If she labors awhile at home, then Dad should handle the child care so that Mom can concentrate on her labor. His responsibilities could include calling for someone to baby-sit whenever mom decides it's time to go to the hospital. He could deal with hospital registration. Also, he should take care of any phone calls announcing the new baby's birth that Mom may be too tired to make.

◆ Even if the first labor went well, it is natural for Mom to feel nervous and apprehensive about this labor. Don't assume she's an old pro and won't need any emotional support. Dads should be prepared for a range of emotions. Each labor is different, just as each child is different, and many mothers can get rattled if things don't proceed at the same pace as the first labor, cautions Sachs. "There are all sorts of anxieties connected with the second labor. There may be pressure to have a boy this time if the first was a girl, for example. Dads can help by providing encouraging words, 'No matter if it's a boy or girl we will love it as much as we do our first,' or 'This labor is going much differently, but you're doing great.'"

◆ Dads should encourage their wives to lay out specifically what he did that worked and didn't work with the last labor. For example: "It really helped when you rubbed my lower back right before I gave birth" or "My feet were freezing by the time I got to the second stage. I could have really used some warm socks" are concrete suggestions that Dad can follow up on in the second labor.

◆ In general, serve as her advocate. Even if you don't always know exactly what to do, the two of you should rely on the bond of intimacy and trust. She should be able to depend on you to help communicate with your doctor and the delivery room staff. Protect her privacy in the labor room. Help her make the best decisions about a new procedure or pain medication.

Does Walking During
Labor Help? Pros and Cons

One area open to debate is the notion that walking—or pacing—during labor will decrease pain and hasten delivery. The latest study published in the *New England Journal of Medicine* in July 1998 found that walking during labor has no effect—good or bad—on labor and delivery. Conducted by Steven L. Bloom, M.D., at the University of Texas Southwestern Medical Center, the study, following over one thousand laboring women, found that walking made no difference in the women's risk of cesareans, in the duration of labor, in the need for pain medicines, or in the babies' health.

Despite these findings, most nurse-midwives and childbirth instructors feel that walking does help the laboring mother. "It's just common sense to be upright during labor and let gravity do its work. The baby, after all, has to come down and out. The more Mom walks, the less chance the baby will get stuck in an unfavorable position. Mom can always get back into bed, but she should have the option of walking," states Marion McCartney.

Marjie Hathaway, director of the Bradley Method of Natural Childbirth in Sherman Oaks, California, agrees. "We encourage laboring women to go for a walk, to take a shower, to squat or to get down on all fours during labor, in order to help make them more comfortable and to help labor proceed at a faster pace."

When mothers are confined to the birthing bed—often hooked up to an electronic fetal monitor—the perceived need for an episiotomy may be increased, according to a study done by Larry Reynolds, M.D., chief of the family medicine department at St. Joseph's Health Centre in London, Ontario. The recent one-year study found that a fixed horizontal birth position can slow labor and inhibit birth while it causes the perineum to tense, which in turn can inhibit pushing and, in the end, result in an episiotomy.

Dr. Nancy Rose feels that women ought to be given the opportunity to walk around if it is more comfortable for them, provided they are monitored intermittently, but says that pacing hasn't been found to actually help a baby be born more quickly or easily.

The main issue seems to be one of comfort. If it feels good, take a walk. But don't feel you must walk if you feel better lying on your side or on your back.

The Latest Developments

Childbirth techniques continue to change and improve over time, so it's worthwhile to keep up on what developments have occurred since your first experience. Here are some of the latest developments since 1996.

• The increased use of *doulas* in the labor room. *Doulas* provide emotional support from midpregnancy through the postpartum period. While they don't take the place of the labor coach, they may offer relaxation techniques, suggest alternate positions, or simply hold the mother's hand. A recent study conducted by Dr. John Kennell, at Houston's Jefferson Davis Hospital, found that mothers reported the continual presence of a *doula* in the labor room—along with the father—made for a less anxious and more effective labor. *Doula* fees range from twelve to eighteen dollars an hour. Call Doulas of North America (DONA), 1–500–325–0472, for information and referrals.

• Two new drugs, misoporsol and prostaglandin, have been found to effectively induce labor. "These drugs can be administered either by oral tablet or vaginal suppository," explains Dr. Rose, "to soften the cervix the night before—and without increasing the rate of C-sections."

➥ TIPS FROM THE TRENCHES ❦

◆ I wish I hadn't labored so long at home. I think it upset my two-year-old to see me in that state. I wanted to spend as much time with him as possible before I went in, but I couldn't concentrate on anything with him around. I know it's supposed to be better to stay at home for as long as possible, but for me, the hospital was more reassuring. And I could focus on my baby without distractions. —*Vicki, Deer Park, New York*

◆ This time, when my labor first started I took a shower and put on some makeup. My husband even took the time to shave before we left for the hospital. It sounds crazy, but it just made me feel better—and my husband wanted us to look good for all the photos. —*Florence, Racine, Wisconsin*

◆ During my first labor, my worst pain was just before my baby's head crowned. I had an incredible burning sensation that I later read is called the "ring of fire." Before my second labor, I told my husband to have wet washcloths ready to apply on my perineum at that time, and it helped immensely. —*Pat, New York, New York*

5

The Birth

My first baby was a scheduled cesarean due to a breech presentation, so for my second I wanted to have a VBAC and
do things as naturally as possible. Boy, what a difference!
My first was at a teaching hospital, and it was like going
into an operation, with twenty med students staring at me.
The second was with a midwife in a birthing center with no
drugs and my husband "catching" the baby. . . . What a
rush!   —*Mary Jane, Eau Claire, Wisconsin*

My first was twenty hours of labor with Demeral and an
epidural; my second was twenty minutes—the baby's head
started to crown in the car! I even had to lie down on the
hospital steps for a double-peaked contraction. The hospital staff came out, put me in a wheelchair, and ran me up to
the delivery room. My husband was still holding the goody
bag when I delivered!   —*Susan, Huntington, New York*

My five-year-old son had been so well prepared to watch the delivery of our daughter that as she slid out into the arms of our midwife, he turned to my husband and said, "Hey, where's the placenta?"   —*Debbie, Louisville, Kentucky*

It seems that no two childbirths are exactly alike. No matter who you talk to, each mother finds marked differences in the two experiences. Our memories of giving birth are probably the most vivid of all our memories. They stay with us forever, it seems, because the experience was such a powerful one.

My grandmother, who at ninety-one was beginning to become forgetful in everyday matters—she left on the range one day, the water running the next, she forgot people's names and got confused over paying bills—never forgot a single detail of her two children's births, which had occurred over sixty-five years earlier. When I was pregnant with Alex, our entire extended family gathered at her Wisconsin farmhouse for a huge party to celebrate her ninety-first birthday, which was to be her last. I remember the two of us taking a walk through the cornfields after dinner, and her reminiscing over the birth of my mother. My grandfather had gone down to the feed store that evening to call for Dr. Roth, the county physician, who—rumor had it—had once tended to the bullet wounds of someone in the Al Capone gang. Dr. Roth rode up the gravel driveway in his buggy, checked my grandmother, and said, "This baby won't get born 'til the morning—let me know when the pains get worse," and promptly stretched out on the couch for a nap. My grandmother told me that she had concentrated on counting the rows of corn outside her bedroom window to ease the contractions. When my uncle was born five years later, Dr. Roth didn't have time to stay overnight. My grandmother said that when Dr. Roth held up my uncle and heard his cry, my grandfather—a man of very few words—came running in from the kitchen and said, "How about that!" as Dr. Roth put him in his arms. My mother remembers having to stay outside on the rope swing until Dr. Roth called her inside.

"You have a baby brother," he said.

"But I wanted a sister," she said. My mother was clearly disappointed.

Dr. Roth sighed. "Well, honey, they were all out of girls."

My mother's response: "Can't we wait 'til they get some more?"

I remember my own two births just as vividly and, like my grandmother, will probably hold on to the details long after I forget other worldly matters.

My first birth was so dreamlike and overwhelming in scope that it seemed to take on religious overtones. I was wheeled into the delivery room so quickly that my hair blew about my face. My husband, apprehensive and anxious, even though everything was proceeding normally, walked beside the gurney saying, "Everything's fine, everything's fine, everything's fine" until the nurse shooed him aside. The delivery room was hushed and quiet and seemed to have a sense of false perspective to it—the lights seemed incredibly bright, the metal instruments overly shiny, the doctors and nurses in masks moving quickly about me. The miracle of Annie appearing seemed to stun my husband and me into silence and tears and awe. The camera lay on another table, forgotten until one of the nurses whispered, "Would you like a picture of the three of you?"

My second birth seemed more like a sports event. After being rushed to the hospital, I had been quickly examined ("Nine centimeters . . . let's go!") and taken to the delivery room. Luckily, my husband had registered the day before or he would have missed the birth, signing papers at admittance.

The same crew was back in the delivery room—same maternity nurse, same technicians, same doctor. No one was gentle with me this time, just boisterous. The fact that I'd done this eighteen months earlier had created a much different delivery room environment. This time my doctor was wearing a black velvet headband and evening clothes—she had been interrupted at a party by a phone call from my husband and, knowing I'd be a fast labor, had just made it to the hospital minutes after I'd arrived. People were talking and cheering me on. "Hurray!" they shouted when Alex slipped out. "Congratulations, a boy this time!" and "Lucky you—one of each!" "Way to go!" said an intern, and actually slapped me on my back! It was as if as a second parent I was given a badge of courage—I had done it all before.

Then one of the nurses said, "He looks just like his sister." As if she could possibly remember. But what an impact that word "sister" made on us! It was the first time it really dawned on my husband and me that we now had two kids—a sister and a brother. We looked at each other in amazement as the thought sank in.

Getting More Anxious About Your Second Birth

Although second births are often easier from an obstetrical point of view, they are not always easier emotionally. A recent study published by the *Journal of Marriage and the Family* found that women become increasingly more anxious concerning this second baby's health at birth—including physical injury or tissue damage—especially if the first baby was born healthy.

"I was terrified that my daughter would have something wrong with her, mainly because my son was born just perfect," admits Lois. "I thought I couldn't luck out twice." Lois's husband, Scott, remembers her first words as their daughter was born. "The first thing she said was, 'Is she all right?' When I assured her she was fine, Lois started crying with relief. We both realized how heavily that fear had weighed on us."

Suzanne, now a mother of three healthy boys, felt similar pangs of anxiety at the birth of her second. "The first time I gave birth I didn't know better, but the second time I had read so much more about the statistics of birth defects and brain damage, and I had heard more delivery room horror stories from other people, so I was really scared. By the time I delivered my third, I was sure something horrible would happen."

Where to Deliver the Second Time Around

This time you may be considering an environment other than the hospital to give birth. There are certainly other options available, and now that you have a sense of what you liked and didn't like about your first birth experience, you can explore the possibility of a home birth or a birthing center as an alternative to the hospital delivery room. Since your first birth, even if it was less than two years ago, both options have been gaining in popularity. Also, now that you're an old pro at birthing, you may feel more confident about trying a less high-tech facility, especially if you had an easy labor and delivery.

Birthing Centers

These often free-standing facilities were developed as an alternative to the hospital environment and as a way to avoid high hospital costs. Birthing centers encourage natural childbirth and have a less structured, more homelike feeling. They screen pregnant women carefully because they can usually handle only low-risk deliveries. If complications do occur, they can move you to a nearby or on-site medical facility. Many birth centers operate within the confines of a hospital, like the Elizabeth Seten Child-bearing Center, which is part of St. Vincent's Hospital and Medical Center of New York. Barbara Schofield, the education coordinator there, reports that many mothers choose a birthing center as a way of having the best of both worlds—natural child-birth with an environment similar to a home birth, but with immediate access to a hospital in case of complications. "We offer analgesics for pain, but not epidurals or spinal blocks. We also offer water births and family-attended births." Schofield also points out that birthing centers are much less expensive than hospitals. A two-day stay costs less than half that of a hospital stay of the same length.

Rick Wade, a spokesman for the American Hospital Association, does caution those who are considering a birthing center to investigate its licensing status. "If a center is affiliated with a hospital, then it is automatically part of that facility's accreditation," he explains. "However, if the center is free-standing, it needs to be licensed by the state's Health Department."

While hospitals are still considered the safest place to have a baby, a 1989 study from the *New England Journal of Medicine* found that birthing centers offer "a safe and acceptable alternative to hospital confinement" for low-risk pregnant women.

Home Birth

If you felt uncomfortable with the high-tech efficiency and antiseptic conditions of a hospital during your first labor and delivery, then you may want to consider giving birth in your home. Home birth is an option becoming more common, especially with second births. One reason is that a home birth is easier on older children.

Although a toddler may sense that something big is going on in the bedroom, he won't have to experience Mom going away. "I loved the idea that I wouldn't have to be separated from my three-year-old," explains Jeannie. "Right after my daughter was born, my mother brought in Eric, and I had both babies in bed with me. I'll never forget that feeling of total completeness. And I wouldn't have been able to have that experience in a hospital setting."

Home births are also a choice for second births simply because pregnant moms are more experienced. "I never would have had the nerve to give birth at home with my first child," admits Greta. "But I was so confident with my second pregnancy that I asked for a home birth. My midwife had two back-up OB-GYNs in case of complications, and I live only a few miles from the hospital, so I really had no qualms."

A home birth can also offer a sense of freedom not found in hospital or even birth center settings. "With my first birth, I felt like a real hospital patient, which I guess I was—strapped down with the fetal monitor, IV attached to my arm," recalls Zelda. At home with my second, I wandered around the house, I went out to the garden and watered the zinnias, I sat with my son and watched some *Sesame Place*, and then I delivered my second son in our king-size bed."

If you're considering having your second delivery at home, there are some points to consider. You may be a candidate for a home birth if you:

- are healthy and at low risk for complications
- are willing to cope with pain without drugs
- live near a hospital
- can take an active role in giving birth
- have access to a certified nurse-midwife as your practitioner (very few obstretricians will preside over a home delivery)

Special Deliveries

Of course, most second births produce healthy babies, despite our worries. Yet not all second births are easy. Although most seem to proceed at a smoother pace because our bodies have gone through it before, there are cases where the second birth will be, not only different, but more difficult.

Breech Birth

Although the causes for a breech birth are not known, they are slightly more common at a second birth—even if the first birth was otherwise normal. If you had a breech presentation at your first birth, you are more likely to have a second breech presentation. That may be because your uterus is shaped in such a way that it might encourage a buttocks-first position.

Sometimes the baby's position can be changed by a method called external version. During an ultrasound exam—usually at about the thirty-seventh to thirty-eighth week of pregnancy—the doctor tries to manually turn the baby by placing his hands on your abdomen. If problems arise, the procedure is stopped and a cesarean section can be scheduled. However, if your first birth was vaginal, then a vaginal birth will certainly be attempted again. If your first was cesarean, then you can still opt for a vaginal birth this time around.

Cesarean Section

According to the American College of Obstetricians and Gynecologists, the cesarean delivery rate in the United States increased from 5 percent to 20 percent between 1970 and 1995. It reached almost 25 percent in 1998 before decreasing recently. In other words, for over a decade, almost one-quarter of all American children have been born by cesarean section. There is much controversy over whether they are performed too often. Critics say C-sections just protect the doctors—it makes for a higher fee, lowers malpractice suits, and hastens delivery. Others insist it is completely safe, produces less pain for the mother during the birth—at least initially, although recovery time is longer—the baby arrives pink and beautifully formed since it didn't have to travel the rocky road of the birth canal, and a scheduled C-section means child-care planning is easier to arrange.

Although we all know cesareans are performed when it is considered not safe for the baby to be delivered through the vagina, a second birth raises other issues. If you did have a C-section the first time around, the reason surrounding that decision will usually form the basis for this second delivery. For example, if your pelvis was too small the first time, it will probably be too small the second time—second babies are often bigger—although there are childbirth instructors in Lamaze and Bradley Method techniques who claim that it is still possible to have a vaginal birth (see VBAC in this chapter) depending on the position the mother holds while pushing or the unique way the second baby fits into the pelvis. If you had a C-section because the baby was in distress or your labor simply didn't progress, then the chances are good that you can try for a vaginal birth the next time around.

In any case, it is helpful to be prepared for both cesarean and vaginal birth. Just because you had a vaginal birth the first time around does not mean you will automatically have another.

"My first delivery was completely normal, and my husband and I were just sailing through my second labor until it came to pushing and then everything stopped," explains Tracy. "The baby was so huge—over ten pounds—that the doctor decided on an emergency C-section. I just didn't expect it, and I really freaked. It turned out fine, but I wish we had been prepared for it before-hand."

When a Cesarean Is Necessary

The American College of Obstetricians and Gynecologists gives the most common reasons why a cesarean birth might be chosen as the safest way to deliver your baby:

- Cephalopelvic disproportion, when the baby's head cannot pass through the pelvis. This is more common with a second birth.
- Fetal distress. This means the baby is having trouble during labor. A common cause is when the umbilical cord gets wrapped around the neck or in some other way is compressed or pinched. Sometimes a doctor can manually adjust the cord. I remember my doctor doing that very thing just as I was pushing out Alex. She told me to freeze, if I could, while she reached in to move the cord. I was amazed at her skill, and seconds later Alex was born. However, not all doctors will attempt this procedure and instead will choose a cesarean.
- Placental problems. If the placenta separates from the uterus wall prematurely and heavy bleeding ensues, or if the placenta is abnormally low in the uterus so that it covers the opening of the cervix—a condition called placenta previa—the baby is usually delivered by cesarean section.
- Abnormal presentation, such as breech birth, in which a baby is born buttocks or feet first, or in other uncommon positions.
- Failure to progress in labor, called dystocia. If, after twenty to twenty-four hours of labor, the cervix stops dilating fully, most doctors will perform a cesarean.

You may also need a cesarean if, since your last vaginal delivery, you've developed certain illnesses such as diabetes or high blood pressure or if you have an active herpes infection on your genitals at the time of your delivery.

Coping with a Cesarean Section

As a certified nurse-midwife, Pam England places a great deal of importance on the benefits of a vaginal birth over a cesarean. CNMs (certified nurse-midwives) cite a quicker recovery rate—which means less time away from your firstborn, instant bonding between mom and infant, more father involvement, less anesthesia, and an all-around healthier baby not exposed to anesthesia.

However, when a C-section is necessary, England stresses that the mom should not feel as if she's somehow "failed" to deliver "the right way." If your child is delivered by cesarean, when old enough, the child should be told that a cesarean is just "another way of being born," without placing any kind of stigma on the event. In addition, she offers these suggestions to make a cesarean a more positive experience:

- Call it a cesarean birth—not section. Don't let the surgical aspects distract you from the focus of welcoming your baby into the world.
- Ask the doctor to cue you when the baby is emerging. Have the dad describe the baby.
- Know that the baby has to go to the warmer for a few minutes after birth, but immediately afterward the baby should be swaddled and placed on the mother's chest.
- Have the father sit close to you and hold you as much as he can during the procedures. Your head and shoulders will welcome his touch.

A Second Cesarean
or a VBAC?

It used to be assumed that if you had a cesarean with your first child, you were automatically scheduled for another one with your second pregnancy. That has changed dramatically in recent years, however, and it is now quite common for pregnant mothers to choose a vaginal birth after cesarean, known as a VBAC.

Are You a Candidate for a VBAC?

In October 1998, the American College of Obstetrics & Gynecology (ACOG) published new guidelines for VBACs. Here are their recommendations:

- A prior low-transverse cesarean delivery
- A clinically adequate pelvis, large enough to accommodate a full-term infant
- No other uterine scars or previous rupture
- Physicians readily available throughout labor, capable of monitoring labor and performing an emergency cesarean delivery
- Availability of anesthesia and personnel for emergency cesarean delivery

The ACOG is still considering factors such as unknown uterine scars, a second breech presentation, twin gestation, and other circumstances. Continued analysis needs to be completed before they make further recommendations.

Dr. Bruce Johnston, OB-GYN at the Mayo Clinic in Rochester, Minnesota, and specialist in VBACs, warns that the greatest risk is uterine rupturing. "If there was a low-transverse incision during the previous C-section—that is, an incision that goes across the lower uterus—then the odds of a rupture are less than half of 1 percent—certainly safe for the mother," he states. "If, however, a C-section was done early on in the pregnancy—at twenty weeks, for example—there isn't enough development in the uterus by that point and the doctor had to make a vertical 'classic incision,' the risk for uterine rupture is much higher, about 10 to 12 percent. Most OB-GYNs will not agree to a VBAC with a patient with a classic incision."

What happens during a uterine rupture? "The uterus basically tears during labor," he states. "It means the immediate removal of the baby by a C-section. Fetal injury, even death, can occur otherwise. Sometimes a hysterectomy is the only way to control the bleeding."

At the Mayo Clinic, Dr. Johnston reports that about 70 percent of pregnant mothers with a prior low-transverse C-section attempt a VBAC; about 50 percent succeed.

"A classic candidate for a VBAC would be a woman with an adequate pelvis who had a breech presentation with her first birth. These women have about an eighty percent success rate with a VBAC," states Dr. Johnson. "Even a woman whose pelvis was too small to give birth vaginally the first time can sometimes manage a vaginal birth the second time, even if the second baby is larger. In fact, about twenty percent of those cases succeed." How can that be if the pelvis obviously does not grow? "It can depend on the position of the baby—it may be facing up the second time as opposed to facing down the first, or it may simply fit better in the pelvis this time," Dr. Johnston explains.

Special Treatment for Moms Having VBACs

A VBAC is considered a special circumstance, and obstetricians treat the laboring mom carefully. This means that the baby's heart is monitored either electronically or internally during the labor. "We treat a VBAC very conservatively," states Dr. Johnston. "A VBAC should take place in a hospital instead of at home or at a free standing birth center because if complications occur we want to be able to intervene immediately."

A 1996 study on VBACs published in the *New England Journal of Medicine* found that women at the highest risk for a failed labor were thirty-five or older, bore a child weighing nine pounds or more, and had had a C-section with their first birth.

Does Having a VBAC Mean No Epidural or Spinal Block?

"Not anymore," states Dr. Johnston. "Years ago the reasoning behind that logic was that an epidural or spinal block would mask any sign of uterine rupturing. But accurate fetal monitoring— either internal or electronic—now shows any aberration. And in reality, the correct dosage level of an epidural is completely safe."

A new needle design within the last couple of years has enabled doctors to administer a spinal block more effectively. "The headache and other after pain associated with this type of regional block occurs when the fluid leaks out," explains Dr. Johnson. "The thinner shape of the new intrathecal needle causes less leakage, which eliminates the headache side effect."

A Second Episiotomy?

As most of us remember all too well, an episiotomy is a small incision made in the area between the vagina and the rectum during delivery when it appears that the baby's head is unable to fit through without tearing the mother's skin and the perineal muscles. The procedure includes using a local anesthetic and requires stitches; recovery can be painful and itchy as the incision heals. For many years hospitals considered episiotomies a routine procedure, and until very recently 90 percent of women were given episiotomies with their first birth.

Second-time mothers, however, tend to have fewer episiotomies—mainly because they've gone through them once before and are often quite vocal about questioning the need for another one.

"Frankly, that was the main reason why I looked for a midwife with my second child," admits Liz. "I didn't really care about all that stuff about nurturing the mother—I just wanted to avoid getting cut again. And it worked. My midwife used K-Y jelly that she had heated up to stretch my tissues, and she had me lie on my side instead of my back, which put less pressure on that area. I delivered my daughter without any tear."

Certified nurse-midwives believe that episiotomies are often not necessary, and that when given the option, a small tear is preferable to an incision because it is not as deep and takes less time to heal. They advocate the continued massage and application of a warm cloth to the perineum as well as coaching the mom on gentle pushing techniques, and alternating prone positions. More and more OB-GYNs are going along with these procedures.

Carolyn remembered sitting in a sitz bath for several hours a day during those first few weeks with her newborn to heal her stitches. "The thought of having to go through that again plus caring for my two-year-old and a newborn just made me crazy!" She spoke to her doctor about her fear of a second episiotomy, saying she'd prefer a small tear than a cut. Her doctor worked with her, having her push at short intervals. "The pushing stage did take a little longer, but in the end I had only a tiny tear that healed up right away."

In Defense of the Episiotomy

"I think, in general, physicians are becoming less dogmatic about the routine use of episiotomies, and as a result there are fewer performed, especially at a second delivery," states Dr. Johnston. "On the other hand, there are some advantages to having the procedure done."

- It saves time when you don't have the luxury of time. "If the baby's head is just too big, and the baby's heart rate is becoming less reassuring, and/or the mother is becoming extremely uncomfortable, a small cut will bring the baby out immediately."
- "An incision is more controlled. Sometimes a cut is preferable to a large tear, especially if a doctor sees the tear will continue toward the rectum to such an extent that it may cause the possibility of future incontinence for the mother. With a cut we can control the placement of the opening."
- With a second episiotomy, the incision can be made along the initial scar. "The second procedure seems to be less painful and it heals faster because of the old scar tissue."

Should Your Child Be at Your Delivery?

There's a growing trend to have an older child present at the birth of his or her sibling, known as a sibling-attended birth, but it's still a controversial topic. Although the American College of Obstetrics & Gynecology does not have specific guidelines concerning sibling-attended births, physicians, child psychologists, midwives, and birthing instructors all have varying positions on the subject. Factors such as your child's age and disposition, the parents' views on nudity and privacy, and the place you'll be delivering all play a part in the decision.

Most couples who opt for a "family" birthing describe it in positive terms. "My six-year-old daughter watched her sister being born last year," remembers Krista. "We did it at home right in our own bed with a nurse-midwife. And when I saw Jenny 'helping' my husband and midwife 'catch' the baby, it was the closest I've ever felt to my family."

Another couple had a total of five family members watching the delivery. "Besides my husband, my parents were there, and my sister was there to watch my son, who was four at the time, in case he wanted to leave the room at any time—which he didn't," says Yvette. "Everyone was there to watch the baby being born. You'd think one of us would have remembered to take photos, but we were all so excited at the time that none of us thought of it 'til afterward." Her husband, Roger, kids her that next time they better make room for an additional person in the delivery room: the photographer.

Not all parents feel a child belongs in the delivery room. Many feel as Darlene did: "The last person I wanted there was my son! Knowing that my mom was staying overnight and dropping him off at preschool the next morning made me a little less stressed. I wanted to be able to concentrate without any distractions."

Suzanne agrees. "My daughter is extremely squeamish—she gets upset when I cut my finger. She'd just freak out in that kind of environment."

When is a sibling-attended birth a viable consideration? Anne C. Bernstein, a child psychologist in Berkeley, California, and author of *Flight of the Stork: What Children Think (and When) about Sex and Family Building*, says that under the right circumstances children can benefit from watching the birth of a sibling. She believes that it is good for a sibling to be included in the experience so that the child can bond instantly with a new brother or sister.

Although opinions differ, most experts believe that children under the age of five or six cannot completely comprehend the birthing experience. Bernstein feels that very young children won't be able to separate from the process. "A child under 3 or 4 years old may be too young to be present at a delivery," she states. "He may not be able to connect what he sees with what is really happening or be able to concentrate on the activity."

Bernstein believes that a sibling-attended birth is better handled at home. "The child can do what he wants if he gets bored— go to his room, watch TV, or read a book. The familiarity of the home environment makes it a less fearful experience, too." Bernstein points out additional factors that can make the experience a positive one for a young child, assuming he has a keen desire to be there.

Prepare the Child Extensively

"He should definitely attend the hospital or birthing center's sibling preparation classes. In addition, he should be prepared for the sights and sounds of childbirth. Has he ever seen Mommy naked before? Does he realize there may be complications such as a Caesarean birth, which would mean he'd be removed from the room at that time?"

Provide a Support Person for the Child

"That person's exclusive role is to support the child at the birth and decide if he needs to be taken from the room."

Psychologist Brad Sachs counsels couples to consider a number of factors before making a decision: "If you see a birth as a family ritual and a natural, organic experience, then you may want to think about a sibling-attended birth," he states. "But both husband and wife must agree that they want their child there. If either feels uncomfortable, then they should decide against it. The next thing to do is discuss the idea with your child. You may say, 'We're thinking of letting you watch your brother being born. What do you think about that idea?' Listen very carefully to his responses and respect his feelings. He may not want to be there, and that's fine. Try not to let your own feelings sway him one way or another.

Umbilical Cord Blood Options

One of the most promising advances in recent medical science is the use of a newborn's umbilical cord blood—especially the stem cells, the same cells found in bone marrow—in order to treat a variety of conditions such as leukemia, lymphoma, myeloma. Although the odds of a child needing his own stem cells are one in one thousand, the cells could be a match for family members. Umbilical cord blood may also prove useful in gene therapy, according to Sandra Wolf, an OB-GYN nurse and childbirth instructor, who works at the Cord Blood Registry in Oswego, Illinois.

"Parents can either bank their infant's cord blood for possible future use, or they can donate the blood to a cord blood foundation, similar to a blood bank," explains Wolf. She suggests that pregnant mothers talk to their doctors about this option long before delivery, since the blood must be saved during the first few minutes after birth. If they want the blood to be stored privately, they must decide at least a month in advance of the birth.

According to the *Journal of Perinatal Education*, private cord blood storage costs approximately fifteen hundred dollars for enrollment and processing, plus ninety-five dollars per year for storage. There is no fee for a donation to a public bank.

⊰ TIPS FROM THE TRENCHES ⊱

⬥ I had my baby at home this time and it was great, except that I had too many people in the room: my mother, my mother-in-law, my sisters, and my five-year-old. It was a party for them, but it was just too much for me. I think if I had it to do over again it would just be my husband and me with our midwife. I really wanted more privacy than I had thought.   —*Heather, Portland, Oregon*

⬥ My VBAC went really well, but I was shocked at how bruised and battered my son looked compared with my cesarean-born daughter. My first thought was, 'Oh no, something's wrong with her! Prepare yourself for a bluish, scrunched up, pointy-headed baby when you give birth vaginally!   —*Lauren, Baltimore, Maryland*

⬥ I think people complain too much about hospital delivery. My girlfriend warned me when I was pregnant the first time about the cold steel, the stirrups, the metal bars, the bright lights. But I opted for the hospital again for my second birth because I just felt safer in that environment. It's good to know if anything goes wrong you're right there to get help.   —*Dawn, Nashville, Tennessee*

6

The Hospital/ Birthing Center Stay

I went into labor about ten at night, but I made sure I got to the hospital just after midnight; I knew from experience that my insurance company counted a day as starting at midnight—and this time I wanted as many days as I could get! —*Marina, Fort Lee, New Jersey*

The best part about delivering at my birthing center was its short-term stay. I came in to deliver at six in the morning and checked out at eight that night! My daughter and son met the same day I delivered! —*Iris, Salt Lake City, Utah*

I said no to "rooming-in" this time. I figured I needed to rest up for what would await me at home—a two-year-old and a husband who can't do laundry! —*Erin, Oakland, California*

I found it a strange, giddy feeling to realize that I now had two children. For so long, I had had this one strong connection with my daughter; now I had this newborn—the strongest bond of all.

Yet that bond didn't seem to interfere with the love I felt for our first. The poets must be right: a mother's intense love is capable of stretching to accommodate another child.

I remember having this powerful urge to call my daughter only moments after Alex's birth. So after the nurse laid Alex in my arms, after my husband and I examined his strong chin, his Roman nose, his full head of hair ("Just like Annie!" exclaimed my husband), we decided to phone home. Our baby-sitter told us that Annie was not sleeping too well without Mom and Dad—it was, after all, 1:30 A.M.—and she was still awake. Kate put Annie on the phone and we told her the news, babbling on because we were so excited, so thrilled, that we wanted her to be a part of it all even though we knew she wasn't able to grasp very much. In fact, Annie, yawning on the phone, only wanted to know when we were coming home.

Less Time for Celebration the Second Time

By the time the nurse got me settled into bed, my husband could only stay a few minutes. We both knew he had to get back home to relieve Kate and tend to Annie. The first time I gave birth we celebrated with champagne—my husband had lain with me in the hospital bed for hours, until the nurse made him leave. *How different this is from my first birth*, I thought as he left. The lack of pampering you get with your second pregnancy really extends through your delivery and hospital stay. Everyone, from the maternity nurses to my husband, seemed much less solicitous this time around.

Already the excitement and anticipation I had felt with my first child seemed to have dissipated more quickly with the arrival of my second. As wonderful as Alex was, I had more mundane matters on my mind. For example, I pictured our house—laundry piled up, the sink stacked with dishes, no sheets to fit the borrowed bassinet. I worried that Annie was missing me, that my husband would be letting her eat too many sweets, that her clothes would be on backwards, that she'd be staying up past her bedtime. The next few months, I knew from experience, would be filed with sleepless nights and zombie-like days. At that moment the future seemed too overwhelming to contemplate.

An hour later, I heard a gurney being wheeled toward my room. It looked like I'd be getting a roommate. I quickly drew the curtain around my bed and pretended to be asleep.

"Nothing is like the magic of the birth of your first child," the nurse was saying as the new mother and father giggled in that almost drunken manner I recognized as the we-did-it-we-really-did-it euphoria experienced right after your first birth.

Through the curtain I heard a paper bag rustle and then the soft pop of a cork.

Him: "You were so great." Clink, clink of glasses.

Her: "No, you were so great."

Him: "No, really, you were so great."

More pouring of champagne.

Her: "No, really. You were so great," Smooch smooch smooch.

The conversation, although kind of sickening, sounded strangely familiar. No doubt my husband and I had said the same words after Annie was born. With Alex's birth, however, the conversation went more like this:

Him: "We can put the bassinet in the hall for the time being."

Me: "We'll need another car seat."

Him: "And those newborn diapers."

Me: "And a double stroller."

Him: "Want a Diet Coke before I go?"

Remembering Your Child
Back Home

No that we ever forgot her. Your older child is probably on your mind as much as your newborn now. After all, this is probably the first time the two of you have been apart. And even though hospital stays are much briefer nowadays, a young child will still feel the absence intensely. A cesarean birth takes a longer hospital stay, and those few extra days can seem like a month to a three-year-old.

The best way to minimize separation anxiety is to keep in touch by phone. I called home twice a day—early morning and late afternoon for the three nights I was in the hospital with Alex. A friend from work brought her Polaroid camera when she came to visit me. She took several photos of Alex and me, and then dropped them off at our house on her way home. Annie seemed to respond to the photos; an older child would enjoy them even more. It is a way of keeping your firstborn part of the "action."

Coping with
Second Baby Blues

The physical and emotional ups and downs we experience after the birth of our second child can be so much more intense than with our first. I call it Second Baby Blues—that vague, guilt-ridden, how-will-I-ever-survive-raising-two-kids emotional roller-coaster ride I was on the day or two after having my son. Not to be confused with postpartum depression, Second Baby Blues has more to do with feelings of being totally overwhelmed as opposed to seriously depressed. And how could we not have those feelings? Here are my own theories for some causes of Second Baby Blues:

When You Know This Second Baby Will Probably Be Your Last

"Bill and I planned on having two children only," says Diane. "And I remember lying in that hospital bed thinking, 'Well, it's over now; we have our family.' One minute I'd feel so relieved that I could get on with my life and get my body back into shape, and then the next minute I'd burst into tears, realizing that I'd probably never be pregnant again, mourning the loss of that chapter in my life."

When You Begin to Think About the Actual Task of Caring for Two Young Children

With your first baby, you may have felt vaguely overwhelmed with the notion of having another human being to care for, but as my neighbor said, "There's a big difference between two adults with one baby and two adults with two babies." A second child can make a new mother panic-stricken at the practical adjustments of caring for two children.

"The night after I had my second baby, I couldn't sleep at all," confesses Sabrina. "I kept obsessing over grocery shopping! I couldn't figure out how I was ever going to manage an infant and a toddler in a grocery cart. Would I carry Caitlan in a baby pack and push the cart with Erin in it? Or should I just use a double stroller? But then where would I put the groceries? It was crazy, but I think it was the panic I felt over having to be responsible for two babies instead of just one."

When You Get Much Less Pampering and General Attention with Baby Number Two

After all, the first time you give birth there're flowers, balloons, telephone calls, friends and relatives dropping by with gifts—maybe even a visit from your Lamaze teacher raving about your fabulous performance during labor and birth. After the second, there's much less hoopla, even from your own husband and family.

"My husband bought me diamond stud earrings after Jaimie was born," says Allison. "Two years later when I had Will, he was so casual about my whole pregnancy and birth; he didn't even bring flowers to the hospital—just my mail! All he talked about was Jaimie's kindergarten teacher conference. I felt so neglected."

When Your Firstborn Makes You Feel Guilty; Having a Visit from Your Older Child Can Be Great for Him but Traumatic for You

"I got really weepy after my husband brought in my four-year-old son to visit me in the hospital," recalls Sally. "Eric was so jealous he wouldn't even talk to me. I thought, *Oh no, I've ruined it for my son!* I knew intellectually that wasn't true, that this kind of behavior was normal, but in my heart I felt so sad that Eric and I would never again have that kind of special closeness you have with your first child."

The good news is that Second Baby Blues usually go away quickly. During those first few days after giving birth your hormones play havoc with your emotions. In addition, your body goes through drastic changes. You feel exhausted from your delivery, your uterus makes a lot of noise getting back in shape, your bottom is uncomfortable at the very least, your breasts may already start to ache in preparation for your milk to come in, and you're eating hospital food. You're in a kind of limbo—waiting for your new life to begin, but unable to take any real action yet.

But after a few days of limbo, things start to work themselves out. Holding your newborn in your arms, letting your firstborn touch him, having both of them in your bed together, communicating with your husband your disappointments and fears, phoning friends who've been through their second childbirth, all help to get over that initial feeling of blues.

I remember my husband calling on the second night with the news that Annie had "helped" put sheets on the borrowed bassinet. I was stunned that my husband had somehow managed to locate and purchase the right size bassinet sheets all by himself! This is a man who's never entered a bedding store in his life. I was greatly encouraged by this feat of daring. If he could do that, anything was possible. I found myself pouring out all my worries, including my resentment over the fact that my roommate got champagne and I got Diet Coke.

"We'll have champagne on your first night home," my husband assured me.

"We'll have to wait till both kids are asleep," I reminded him.

"Wow, did you hear that? You said 'kids.' That's the first time I heard that. Wow," he repeated.

Wow, indeed.

Of course, it must be noted that if the blues you're experiencing in the hospital become severe or do not go away after a few days, you may be experiencing postpartum depression (see chapter 7).

Dad's Second Baby Blues

Let's not forget about Dad feeling overwhelmed at the birth of his second child. "Both parents can be feeling extremely overwhelmed those first few days after the birth of their second child," states David Krauss, Ph.D., a Cleveland psychologist who specializes in fathering issues. "But the added financial responsibility usually hits the father the hardest. He is more likely to focus on practical matters, such as child-care costs, housing needs, and other practical matters."

Ralph, a high school teacher, felt that financial burden immediately after his second daughter's birth. "Even though my wife works full time too, I felt like it was my job to protect my new family financially. Those first few days I spent alone with our son while my wife was in the hospital were the toughest. And as I looked down the road all I could see was teaching summer school and home tutoring for the rest of my life."

In addition, fathers are also burdened by the sudden responsibility back home. "Suddenly Dad has to leave his wife at the hospital or birthing center and manage caring for their older child—whose behavior may not be exemplary with Mom gone—and often has to go to work too. A father becomes kind of a single parent for a day or two—usually on very little sleep."

Krauss suggests that both mothers and fathers try to talk through their anxieties as soon as possible. "So often spouses think each other will magically know what's on the other's mind. It doesn't work that way, especially in those first few days after the birth of your second child when both parents are going through an adjustment. It's really important to establish an open dialogue in order to begin the process of communication that you'll both need in the weeks to come.

How Long Will You Be Staying?

Hospital Stays

If you're recovering at a hospital, you may have been surprised to learn that your stay will probably be significantly shorter than when you were there for your first—especially if that was more than a few years ago. Insurance companies and HMOs have steadily shortened hospital stays for vaginal births—from over a week in the days when our mothers gave birth to only twenty-four hours today. Hospital stays for cesarean births have also been significantly reduced to less than forty-eight hours.

In fact, managed care groups had so reduced hospital stays for mothers that women's groups began to lobby for longer stays. And according to a 1998 article in the *Journal of the American Medical Association*, physicians were compensating for these policies by classifying more newborns as sick, thereby allowing for longer hospital stays to be reimbursed by insurance carriers.

Health Plans Required to Grant Longer Stays

Bonnie Connors, director for maternal care at the American Association of Hospitals in Washington, D.C., believes mothers should be made aware of a new law passed to protect maternal hospital stays. "The Newborn and Maternal Protection Act of 1996 was passed by many states to provide longer hospital stays for mothers," states Connors. "But in October of 1998 it became a federal act, protecting women in all states. It reads that health plans must have a provision that allows women a minimum forty-eight-hour stay for vaginal births and a minimum ninety-six-hour stay for C-sections." The law recognizes the basic right of mother and physician to make decisions about the aptness of discharge timing.

Despite this law, some moms are very happy to leave the hospital as soon as possible, especially knowing they have another child at home. "I was in a much bigger hurry to get home after my second baby," remembers Clarissa. "I had never been separated from my toddler before; I think it bothered me more than it bothered him."

Amanda remembers being inspired watching Diana, princess of Wales, emerging from the hospital—looking glamorous and radiant—less than twenty-four hours after the birth of her second son, Harry. "I thought, well, if she can do it so can I!"

Wendy, on the other hand, saw the hospital stay as a kind of minivacation before she went home. "A private room, phone, TV, magazines, breakfast in bed, and friends dropping over. What more could I want?" she asked. "Besides, I knew from experience what the next few months would be like, so I decided to enjoy the last bit of pampering I'd be getting for a while."

Birthing Center Stays

In general, birthing centers are very short-term stays, often keeping the mother overnight only—and sometimes less than that. Some second-time mothers, anxious to get back to their older child at home, will opt for this kind of setting. The Elizabeth Seten Birthing Center in Manhattan keeps to an average twelve-hour stay, reports coordinator Barbara Schofield. "A twenty-year history of short-term stays demonstrates that early discharge works," she says. She adds that birthing centers often use a more extensive follow-up evaluation than hospitals. At Seten, for example, mothers may get a visit from a visiting nurse and a call from a lactation consultant on the second day. A physician may call on the fifth or sixth day; and on the seventh day, mother and baby often make a return office visit.

Does "Rooming-In" Make for a Happier Baby?

Often mothers find it easier to breast-feed their newborn if he or she "rooms" with her in the same room. On the other hand, some second-time mothers decide to recuperate alone in their room, gathering strength for the upcoming sleepless nights. However, rooming-in might be better for your infant if you plan on breast-feeding. A study in the *Journal of the American Medical Association* found that breast-feeding frequency was significantly higher among infants rooming-in than those not. It also found that babies gained more weight and needed less milk supplements when they roomed-in with their mothers.

Recovering from Your Second Birth

I was surprised to discover that recovering from my second delivery took longer than from my first. The uterine cramps I had experienced with Annie were so minor I didn't even ask for aspirin, but after Alex was born I demanded something stronger. I had assumed that since my body was used to the stretch, so to speak, that I'd be bouncing back in no time.

"Not true," says Mayo Clinic's Dr. Bruce Johnston. "The very fact that your body has gone through this before—that those tissues and muscles have been stretched once, causes them to take a little longer to go back. In addition, uterine cramping tends to be more severe after a second delivery, although we don't really know the reason for this."

The good news is that if you had a second episiotomy, it was probably a smaller incision this time, so the recovery will be quicker. You may have been able to give birth without an episiotomy or with a small tear, which can also heal quicker than an incision.

Although it varies from mother to mother, second C-sections in general may take a bit longer to recover from. "There is the potential for more discomfort because there's more scar tissue; the surgery is trickier because it's along the line of the original incision," Dr. Johnston states. "On the other hand, knowing you have another child to care for may make you get on your feet faster, despite the fact that you won't be able to carry your firstborn for the first few weeks."

Introducing Your Baby to Your Ex-Baby

Years ago hospitals had strict rules against children visiting the maternity ward. Officials believed that children could infect newborns, that they would make too much noise, disturbing mothers and other patients, and that they would be traumatized by the experience.

These days, however, hospitals have been forced by consumer demand and the competition—like birthing centers, which encourage family visitations—to loosen their rules. As a result, almost all hospitals allow children in the maternity ward and have liberal visitation hours as well.

Whether or not to have your child visit you in the hospital is a personal decision however. You may think your child is too young to come to the hospital. I decided that it was better for Annie, at eighteen months, to go about her regular routine than to come to the hospital. You may decide against having your child visit you at the hospital or birthing center because you feel that your child will get upset separating from you again at the end of the visit. But the American College of Obstetrics & Gynecology believes that children who visit their mothers respond better to their mothers and their siblings than those who do not visit. Here are their recommendations to consider before bringing a child to the maternity ward:

+ The child should not have been exposed recently to infectious diseases such as chicken pox.
+ The child should not have a fever, cough, or other symptoms that are contagious.
+ The child should be prepared in advance for the visit.
+ The child should be watched by a responsible adult during the entire visit.

Sometimes visits don't go as well as expected. Some children are bored by the whole experience, some are fascinated with their new siblings, others show anger toward their mother. It's important to keep your expectations in check. Gayle, mother of two boys, remembers her three-year-old's visit to the hospital.

"I did everything wrong," she admits ruefully. "My parents and sister were there—which was too much distraction for Matt. And I was so desperate for the boys to 'bond,' that I pushed too hard to make Matt 'like' little Jack. I was holding Jack when Matt came in the door, sort of putting him in Matt's face—and right off the bat he was mad at me. I should have kept Jack in his own bassinet and just focused on Matt for a while. My husband had dropped off Matt on the way to work and my parents took him home, which I think also got him a little discombobulated. Looking back, Daddy should have taken him home. I'd also suggest having no other visitors when your child comes the first time."

Breast-Feeding in the Hospital

If you breast-fed your first baby, you will be able to recognize the signs of your milk "coming in." With your first birth, this may have happened around the third day. With your second birth, it will probably take less time. In fact, a study done by the Maternity Center Association of New York showed that second-time moms get their milk almost a day earlier than first-time moms. This means that your newborn, able to nurse earlier, may become more content and fonder of feeding.

La Leche League, the international breast-feeding organization, believes milk comes in for first- or second-time mothers the same way: as a direct result of how quickly and frequently they put their newborn to their breast. "It may be that second-time mothers are more relaxed and experienced with nursing and as a result their newborns are put to the breast sooner, causing milk to come in sooner," says Cecilia, a local La Leche leader.

The American Academy of Pediatrics, in August 1998, released new guidelines for breast-feeding, confirming what many mothers already knew: that breast feeding of newborns should begin as early as the first hour of birth, and that it should be the only source of nutrition for the first year of life—and longer if mother and baby so desire. This includes sick and premature newborns as well.

The benefits of breast-feeding are well-documented. There's strong evidence that it decreases the incidence of serious diseases like meningitis and botulism as well as lower respiratory, middle ear, and urinary tract infections in infants. It may protect against sudden infant death syndrome, diabetes, allergies, lymphoma, colitis, and other digestive illnesses.

Breast-feeding helps Mom recover faster too. Nursing mothers have less bleeding and improved bone strength. Their uteruses contract sooner, and they return to their prepregnancy weight sooner. They are also less likely to develop ovarian and breast cancers.

Despite these findings, it may become a real challenge for you to find the time and the opportunity to nurse your baby while caring for your older child as well. That's why it's so important to use your one-on-one hospital time with your newborn to establish an immediate nursing bond with your baby.

Second-time nursing is easier because it's more familiar. I remember sitting in the nursery with Annie trying to get the hang of nursing while the nurses helped me. Out of the corner of my eye I saw, across the hall, a mother calmly breast-feeding her newborn while leafing through some preschool drawings her toddler had made. "How will I ever manage that?" I wondered at the time. However, when my son was born it all came back to me, and before long he was breast-feeding while I watched my roommate struggling with her first attempts with nursing.

Despite the emotional ups and downs and all the practical concerns you and your husband have now that you have two children, it's important to sit back and try to get a sense of perspective on your new situation. You and your husband have truly been twice blessed and for that you should rejoice.

≫ TIPS FROM THE TRENCHES ⃗

◈ When you phone your older child from the hospital or birthing center, don't talk about your newborn so much. My son didn't really want to hear about her blue eyes or black hair. He wanted to talk to me about himself. I suggest asking questions about his day—and just listening. Wait for him to ask about the baby.

—*Rita, Caledonia, Wisconsin*

❀ I had my husband pick up a little gift for my two-year-old so when he came for his first visit at the hospital, we gave him a "present from your new brother." It really helped him feel better.

—*Bonnie, Park City, Utah*

❀ Make sure your husband brings your older child to the hospital when it's time for you to be discharged. I think it makes them feel like they're a part of the family. I had my four-year-old pick out my newborn's "going home clothes"; she even "helped" put on my newborn's hat.   —*Adalis, Bloomington, Minnesota*

 III

A Family of Four

7

The First Weeks

When I saw my two-year-old son stand next to our newborn in her baby carrier, I was amazed at his size. Compared with her, he suddenly looked huge—a giant!

—*LaVerne, Dover, Delaware*

The first thing I saw when I got home was the piled-up laundry basket at the foot of the stairs. I almost collapsed right then and there at the thought of the work that lay ahead of me. —*Dana, Charleston, West Virginia*

My mother greeted me at my front door with my daughter. My husband carried our newborn son, my daughter stared at the baby, I held the baby clothes, sort of dazed, and for a minute, everyone just stood there in the foyer, frozen. "What should we do now?" we all wondered.

—*Sue Ann, Asheville, North Carolina*

Coming Home

The day you come home with your newborn is a day fraught with anxiety and joy, panic and thrills, exhilaration and raw fear. It is the day the roller-coaster ride begins. You are now a family of four, and that realization can sometimes be just too much for a new mother. This emotional upheaval, combined with the greater physical discomfort associated with a second birth, can make a new mother feel completely overwhelmed during her first week home.

Most moms will say that despite the fact that they're used to caring for a newborn, the adjustment to home life seems more difficult because they have their firstborn to care for as well.

Kabia, a mother of two school-aged children, remembers that first week well. "I thought it would be a piece of cake this time," she laughs ruefully. "But although I was more confident in breast-feeding and bathing my second baby, I found it difficult to give attention to my three-year-old at the same time. My husband was away on business for the last part of that first week; I was so sure I could handle the whole situation that I had given him my blessing. I had always prided myself on my clean house and organized kitchen. Well, I tried to keep everything in order, run after our very active son, and care for our newborn. By the end of the first week I started to bleed again, just from trying to maintain the house, my son, and my new daughter. I had to stay in bed for the second week just to recuperate from the first week."

Corien agrees that the first week home can be the most exhausting part of the adjustment for a family of four. "Thank God my best friend, Erica, was there to smooth the way that first week," she confesses. "My husband brought us home from the hospital, but really just had time to bring in the car seat before he had to go back to work! Erica had gone through adjusting to two children a few years ago, so she really knew what to do. Mainly, she made me rest whenever there was a lull in the general activity!"

There never seemed to be any downtime during my first week home. My mother came to stay with us the second or third day after I came home from the hospital, and until then there was mass pandemonium. What a difference from my firstborn's homecoming! Annie had slept through the ride home and during the first few hours in the house. I remember laying her in the middle of our king-size bed, and my husband and I curling up next to her on either side. We must have watched her sleeping for an hour or so. For a while life was so peaceful!

After Alex's arrival, there never seemed to be a minute of peace. I would put Alex in the borrowed cradle while my husband sat Annie on the potty. Then Alex would wake up screaming. Then Annie would start crying because the baby was crying. Annie began to regress. She began sucking her thumb again and went back to diapers, even though she had been progressing well with toilet training.

Annie was very curious about Alex, but not exactly cheerful about him. My mother remembers Annie scowling a lot during that first week. She would rock the cradle so hard that it would wake up Alex.

My husband tried to keep Annie occupied whenever it was time for me to nurse Alex, but several times she got away and stood in the doorway of our bedroom, staring dolefully at the two of us in the rocking chair. Once I dozed off for a few minutes and awoke startled to find Annie peering down into my blouse with a puzzled expression as Alex suckled peacefully.

Zombie Days, Zombie Nights

How do you cope with all the chaos of that first week home with a newborn and a young child? The first thing to do, according to Atlanta-based family therapist Elizabeth Ellis, is to let go. "Let go of the laundry, the kitchen counters, the bed making, the meal preparation," advises Ellis. "It is really impossible for second-time mothers to balance the care of a newborn with the care of their firstborn and still be able to manage keeping up a household— especially during that first week. Concentrate on your two children and forget about housekeeping."

Getting Help

Besides leaving the housework to others, what other ways can mothers cope with the zombie days and nights of the first week? Experts tell us that there are ways to ease the difficult transition into second-time parenthood. Here are some coping strategies:

Hire a postpartum doula. Although *doulas* are trained to assist mothers in labor, delivery, and postpartum, about 15 percent are specially trained to help mothers during the first weeks and months after delivery. According to Sandra Szalay, a nurse practitioner and president of Doulas of North America (DONA), postpartum *doulas* receive five days of additional training on the needs of a new family, care of mother and baby, breast-feeding techniques, and sibling issues.

"Second-time mothers can gain special benefits from using a postpartum *doula*," says Szalay. "Women are having families at a later age, and the birth of their second child obviously makes them older still. We're seeing more forty-year-old, second-time moms using *doulas* to help ease the workload."

Doulas can also help couples who have no network of extended family living nearby. "Years ago Grandma or Aunt Sue would stay with Mom the first week or so," states Szalay. "Unfortunately, with families moving more and grandparents often unavailable, new mothers are sometimes just left to their own devices. That's where a *doula* comes in."

Even if a mother does have extended family close by, she may still opt to use a *doula* with her second child. Some *doulas* will agree to baby-sitting duties provided they are set up in advance. "My mother stayed with me after Eric was born; but when Horst was born, I decided it was just too much for my mother to run after Eric and look after me and Horst at the same time. My husband was working a double shift at the time, and I don't know what I would have done without our *doula*. My mom still came over, but it was to pick me up and take me out for lunch! I could relax because I had someone to watch over the boys."

Debra Brewster, a postpartum *doula* in Massachusetts, explains that her duties for a second-time mother include helping the older sibling adjust to the new baby and to his or her new role as an older brother or sister. "Often a second-time mother is more specific about what she wants me to do because she's been through postpartum before. So I'll come into the home prepared to follow her wishes. My role, as always, is to fill in the gaps but not take the place of the mother. I try to make life easier for her." The length of time spent with a family ranges from one week to over a month. The number of hours and days can be negotiated. For example, a *doula* may be hired for six four-hour visits or ten three-hour visits. Some work nights and can help with night feedings. Costs average from eighteen to twenty-five dollars an hour, depending on location. It is interesting to note that some insurance companies will cover up to twenty hours of *doula* visits, and birth centers sometimes include *doula* hours with their childbirth packages. Listed below are some of the duties you might ask of a postpartum *doula*:

- Maintain the older child's routine.
- Provide information on breast-feeding or infant bottle-feeding.
- Bathe and diaper the newborn.
- Run errands, do grocery shopping.
- Advise on the mother's postpartum pain relief.
- Support and interact with the father.
- Take the older child for a walk or to the park.
- Teach the older child how to handle the newborn.
- Throw in a load of laundry if asked.
- Help with light housekeeping.
- Prepare meals and healthy snacks with the older child's "help."

"Our jobs as *doulas* are to maximize the time with your new-born and your older child," says Brewster. "We try to reduce the stress of parenting with nonmedical care, to 'mother the mother,' especially during that first week home."

For information and referrals, call the National Association of Postpartum Care Services (PO Box 1012, Edmonds, WA 98020) 800-45-DOULA.

Cut a Deal with Dad. Remember family therapist Darcy Pattison's wise words in chapter 2, when she advised sitting down with your husband and talking through what worked and what didn't work when your first child was born? She advised coming up with a plan to get through that first week by dividing chores and custodial duties, including taking turns caring for both infant and older child. Now is the time to put your plan into action.

"One reason the second baby's homecoming can be smoother than that of the first is that both spouses have a better sense of what to expect," says Pattison. "While each circumstance is dif-ferent, you can pretty much predict what jobs each of you do best.

You may know, for example, that your husband is okay with giving dinner and a bath to the older child as long as you let him sleep through the night on weeknights. Or your husband may offer to walk the halls with your newborn to get him to sleep, while you cuddle and read a story to your oldest."

Roberta and her husband, Hank, found that by talking through specifics they were able to avoid the feelings of anger and resentment they had both experienced the first time around. "This time, the first thing we did was negotiate the nighttime feedings. That was what we used to fight about the most when our first was born. He felt that since he worked he should be able to sleep. I, of course, felt that I worked too. So this time I made a deal with him. I agreed that the first week I'd be responsible only for getting up with the baby. He agreed that I'd have two free hours, each day, from 6:00 to 8:00 A.M., for myself. If our toddler had a nightmare, it was Hank who would go to him. Naturally I got up several times a night with the baby to breast-feed, but my reward was knowing that time that day when I could rest, take a shower, or just talk on the telephone. Knowing that I'd have that to look forward to kept me from hating Hank as he snoozed at three in the morning."

Hank found it helpful to know what his wife needed those first few days at home. "I wanted to help my wife during this crazy period. I knew she'd be exhausted. But fathers are affected by the adjustment of another baby too, and unless our wives communicate their own needs, we're lost," he explains. "For example, when Roberta told me that my bringing her a glass of juice while she was nursing made her feel more cared for, I was happy to do it. And it made me feel less guilty when I slept through a night feeding."

The most important way to enlist your husband's help is to communicate your specific needs. Try to figure out what part of that initial adjustment makes you the most anxious, the most crazy, the most exhausted, and then try to think of what things your husband could do to calm you down, to give you some breathing space.

When my husband and I "duked it out" over duties that first week with both kids, we ended up with a pretty fair contract. My husband's job was to supply dinner the first week. That could mean take-out, thawing out frozen dinners my mother had made, or cooking his recipes—which, by the way, were my favorite choice. He is great at cooking Italian. When he cooked, I loaded the dishwasher. Part of the deal was that I couldn't offer any suggestions. "No editorializing" was the way he put it. He'd also do all the laundry the first week, provided that I put everything in the laundry basket and set it at the basement door. We took turns cleaning the house. He also took on potty duty with Annie, which mainly meant spending long periods of time hanging out in the bathroom—an activity my husband did anyway, as I reminded him. Those two areas freed me up to concentrate on the main custodial care of Annie and Alex.

And remember, this time around you both have to consider your firstborn's needs. The deal you cut should be fair to both of you and to your older child. And although a newborn will be more needy of Mom that first week, try to make time for your firstborn even when you're consumed with your newborn. Despite our careful planning, I started feeling guilty about not spending enough time with Annie. I was so busy nursing Alex and trying to get him to sleep (he was—and still is—a much lighter sleeper than his sister was) that I had no time for all the little things I used to do with Annie before her brother was born. We used to have a long, drawn-out bedtime ritual—close the blinds together, brush our teeth, brush the teeth of assorted stuffed animals, read several stories, and so on.

My husband's bedtime ritual was dramatically shorter—and I could hear her complaints while I sat in bed nursing Alex. "Where's Mommy?" she'd ask. "She's busy with Alex," my husband would say. Dead silence. I would be filled with despair and guilt at that moment. I was certain that I'd never be able to give enough love to two children. Luckily, I had a very good friend who had managed to raise four loving, well-adjusted children, so I knew it had to be possible to manage with just two.

Allow friends to help. That's a tough one, isn't it? Many women find asking for help so difficult that they would rather suffer in silence. But believe me, this is not the time to suffer alone. Let your friends, neighbors, and relatives step in. Think of it this way: You make them feel good about themselves if you let them do you favors. In fact, you do them a favor by letting them help you.

So who do you ask for help—and, more important, what do you ask them to do? Here is a sample of what some mothers answered to that age-old question: "Can I help at all?"

- Bring over a casserole.
- Take Susie to the park or playground.
- Come over for an hour and let me sleep.
- Stay with the baby so I can spend thirty minutes helping James with his homework.
- Bring me some books or magazines or videos from the library.
- Write my thank-you notes for me—but don't tell anyone!
- Walk our dog, or better still, stay with both children so I can walk the dog.

Often when friends are asked to perform a specific task, they are happy to do it. It's all in the communication.

Listen to Other Mothers' Stories. When we're going through something that, at the time, seems impossible, it's a good idea to hear how others went through the same situation. I found it so comforting to hear the sometimes difficult, sometimes hilarious, stories from my friends and acquaintances about when they had their second child. My friend with the four well-adjusted children had gothic horror stories to tell about the first week home with all four. She remembers that bringing home the second child was the hardest because it was the biggest adjustment combined with the biggest guilt trip. "By the time my fourth was born, I stayed in bed the whole first week, wearing the same sweatpants. I tried to conduct all business from my bed—I think I even changed a few diapers there. I highly recommend it," she advises.

I received many pearls of wisdom at the lunch table in our school's faculty room, some of which I now pass along to you:

- Sometimes you will hate your husband for not being born with breasts.
- Having your mother or mother-in-law there to help is not necessarily always helpful.
- Your oldest child, even if he or she is still just a toddler, knows instinctively what buttons to push in the guilt department.
- You don't have to answer the door when a well-meaning neighbor comes over to "see the baby" at the same magic moment that both number one and number two are asleep at the same time.

What to Expect from Your Firstborn

No matter how well you think you know your child, it isn't until your firstborn and your newborn have spent a few days under the same roof that you can begin to get an idea of the older child's reaction to a new sibling. My friend Kathleen was so shocked at the aggressiveness of her firstborn daughter, Sarah—a delightfully happy and gentle three-year-old up until the arrival of her sister—that she seriously considered taking her to therapy. "She walked right over and smacked Kate across the head," Kathy remembers. "Then she grabbed my husband and me by our sleeves and actually tried to pull us out of the nursery!"

Gloria and Victor witnessed the opposite reaction with their four-year-old son. "Alex was accustomed to being the center of the universe in our family," confesses Victor. "So we were prepared for outright hostility the day we brought home Gabrielle. But Alex was thrilled! He wanted to help diaper and feed her right from the start. He saw her as another toy for himself, I think." Gloria adds, "Once Alex realized that Gabby slept and cried a lot, he became a bit disenchanted and bored with the whole idea of his new sister."

Jealousy Is Natural

We all know children are unpredictable in general, and this situation is sure to bring more surprises than usual. Your firstborn may be disappointed that the new baby isn't an instant playmate. The baby may even be the wrong sex. No matter how much you prepare your oldest, he or she will probably still be annoyed by a sibling's crying and sleeping. But above all, your oldest will certainly notice that he or she is not getting the attention the child was used to before Mom brought home a baby. That's when the firstborn starts getting jealous.

To better understand how your oldest feels when introduced to a sibling, psychologists use the following comparison: Picture your husband coming home one day and saying, "Honey, I love you so much I wanted another wife just like you. She's moving in now, she's sharing your room, and for a while I'm going to be really busy taking care of her. I know the two of you will get along just great and that you'll love each other forever."

Wise parents neither ignore jealousy nor denounce it. It's better to acknowledge it: "You feel angry that Mommy has to feed the baby instead of reading you a story." Assure your firstborn that although you love the baby, you love him or her just as much. I finally got my daughter to understand this strange concept by asking her who she loved more: Mommy or Daddy. She was stumped and finally replied, "I love you both the same way." *Aha*, I thought, *she's beginning to get it.* The younger your firstborn is, the more apt the child will be to feel the weight of the green-eyed monster. Here are some ways to minimize the jealousy bug in the initial days at home with the new baby:

◆ The most effective way to curb your older child's jealousy is to spend one-on-one time with him or her. Try to spend at least fifteen minutes a day "floor time" —uninterrupted, unorganized time alone with your oldest. The baby should be in another room sleeping or with Dad. Don't suggest a game or reading; let your child choose the topic of conversation or the activity.

◆ Give your older child a new privilege. Even being allowed to stay up fifteen minutes later before going to bed will make a child feel the advantage of being the firstborn. Letting a child watch a special TV show, use a new computer game, or ride his or her bike down to the corner will underscore the child's new role as big brother or sister. If your child is old enough, let the child answer the phone or have him or her make the calls to announce the birth to friends and acquaintances.

◆ Consider getting your child a pet. This is only for animal lovers, of course, but if you were considering a pet in the past, this would be the right time to do it. A pet can comfort the older sibling and will give him or her someone to love while adjusting to the attention the new baby is getting during the first few weeks. As wonderful as these sentiments are, I have to add a caveat here: bringing an untrained puppy, for example, into a home with a new baby can mean even more work and chaos that first week. In my case, as much as I love animals, I would have probably jumped out the window if I had one more soul to care for the first week. Experts notwithstanding, I suggest a goldfish as the ideal carefree pet.

Regression Is Also Natural

Don't be surprised if your "grown up" toddler or preschooler suddenly goes backward in progress: A potty-trained three-year-old may demand diapers again, a toddler may throw away a drinking cup and grab the newborn's bottle, a kindergartner may suddenly be unable to sleep through the night. All these behaviors are completely normal the first few weeks. After all, your firstborn observes how much attention the new baby gets and may figure out that by becoming a baby again he or she may get the same nonstop care. Regressing back to baby behavior is a child's way of reminding you that your firstborn still needs Mom's and Dad's care too.

My neighbor, Jean Marie, remembers that her three-year-old daughter, completely potty trained for over a year, suddenly wanted to wear diapers after she saw her mother diaper the baby. "Initially I panicked. Just the thought of two babies in diapers threw me for a loop," she admits. "But then I went along with it and diapered her over her clothes, stressing that we were playing baby. She went around like that for a day or two and then got tired of it." Jean Marie's advice is to be patient and let the regressive behavior work its way out.

That advice worked for Renee, whose two-year-old nagged her to drink from the baby's bottle. Finally, one day after a feeding.

Renee handed her the bottle. She took a swallow and wrinkled her nose. "Bad!" she said, and never asked again.

Even an older sibling may regress by becoming more babyish. A child may adopt a whining tone, throw a minor tantrum, or display acute anxiety by asking countless questions about the baby.

By allowing your child to act out babyish, sometimes outrageous behavior without interference, that child will know that you accept him or her without judgment and will work out these feelings in a natural, unhampered way. Your firstborn may even surprise you with new maturity after the dust settles. Studies show that after the birth of a sibling, the firstborn—after the initial regression—will often show a growth spurt of development.

Helping Your Firstborn to Adjust

You can minimize the upheaval in your firstborn's life by keeping the child's daily life as normal and peaceful as possible. Here are some strategies that worked for second-time moms during that first crazy week home.

No Unnecessary Visitors the First Few Days

It sounds harsh, but your new family of four needs private time to get acquainted. I remember having to entertain a well-meaning coworker the third day I was home. She stayed for two hours while I sat there, my bottom still aching, my daughter on my lap trying to get my attention, and my newborn fussing in his infant seat. Boy, do I regret opening the door that day.

Your firstborn needs a lot of attention, especially if you've been gone for a few days. Let the answering machine screen telephone calls too so that you can focus on your oldest child.

Maintain the Child's Routine As Much As Possible

Try to have your firstborn's meals ready at roughly the same time, even though that will not be easy. Maybe Dad can hold the baby so that Mom can make Billy's favorite grilled cheese sandwich. If that's too much for Mom, she can just sit at the kitchen table while Billy eats graham crackers. It's the physical presence that counts.

If your firstborn goes to day care or kindergarten, keep the routine too. Experts tell us that routines, especially in very young children, can soothe their anxieties and actually bring them comfort. This is very important during the first week, when it will seem to you that there is no routine. Days and nights become a blur to parents when the inevitable sleep deprivation hits. Yet for your older child, maintaining bedtime rituals, bath times, and story reading will help make for an easier adjustment.

Let Your Oldest Help

Parenting experts agree that your firstborn will begin to bond with a sibling much sooner if he or she is able to take an active role in the baby's daily life. Depending on age, a child can "help" with small tasks—under your close supervision, of course. Even a two-year-old can fetch a diaper and choose a new stretchie. Older children can take part in bottle-feeding, cradle rocking, burping, and changing diapers. Let your firstborn hold the baby—on the floor with pillows for support. Show the child the baby's soft spot and the umbilical cord stump and explain that he or she must be very careful when handling the new baby.

Remember, however, never to leave the baby alone with your toddler—not even for a minute. Despite a child's good intentions, your older child could inadvertently harm your infant. We've all heard stories from experienced mothers of two who describe their toddlers and preschoolers picking up a sibling to give the baby a bath or playing hide-and-seek with a pillow over the baby's face, or dressing the baby up in "play clothes."

One mother I know used to bring the baby in an infant seat into the bathroom while she showered because her four-year-old had previously tried to "help" her brother by feeding him some M&M's. No harm was done, thank goodness, but the mother never left the two of them alone after that.

Separate the Baby's Sleeping Area from Your Older Child's

Ideally, of course, the baby and your firstborn should have separate rooms; at the very least they should have separate sleeping areas those first few weeks. This may seem minor, but having the baby's area set up before you come home from the hospital keeps a sense of order and harmony during this first week (see chapter 3). Seeing where the baby sleeps and where the baby's diapers will be changed is a way of making your firstborn see how the new baby will fit into the family structure. That's not always feasible if your living area is small. When Alex was born, we were living in a small two-bedroom cottage. We planned on putting both children in the same bedroom, but during the first few weeks, we kept Alex in a borrowed cradle in our bedroom. We even put the changing table in our room. That way Annie kept her bedroom to herself during the initial adjustment period. We figured she had enough to contend with, without sharing her bedroom right off the bat.

Sometimes there's even less room for the baby. I know of one mother who set up a crib and changing table in her dining room for the first week. She had her five-year-old help get the crib and changing table set up, but reminded her that after the baby got used to a bedtime routine, they'd be sharing a room. Preparing your oldest ahead of time gives him or her a chance to get used to a growing family.

Remind a Child That He or She Is Special

We may say "I love you" a hundred times a day, but sometimes actions speak louder than words. Showing your firstborn that he or she is special with specific deeds will reinforce that love. For example, when it's feasible, let the baby cry a bit while you let your older child finish a sentence, or wait until you've finished the story you're reading until you run to the crib.

I found that by getting out the photo album and showing Annie pictures of her as an infant helped her realize that I *did* lavish the same care and attention on her as I was doing with Alex. I showed her a picture of me nursing her, of me bathing her in a rubber tub in the kitchen sink, and of us sleeping together in my husband's and my bed.

Although it never hurts to tell your child you love him or her, try to be more specific in your communications that first week. Show gratitude when your oldest helps with the baby, confide that it's so great to have a "big boy or girl" who doesn't need diapers or a bottle, whisper that you remember when the child was a baby and how beautiful he or she was. And then let yourself remember too.

Breast-feeding Number Two

It took a little work on my part to get the hang of breast-feeding, but by the time Alex was born I felt like an old pro. However, for me, nursing always felt like a private matter. Although I admired women who could suddenly plop down in the park or in a restaurant, take out a breast, and go to it, I was forever looking for places to nurse behind closed doors. At shopping malls, for example, I discovered that the changing rooms at the Gap were great places to breast-feed, as long as there was a lock on the door.

At any rate, you can imagine my chagrin when, after dozing off while nursing Alex that first week, I woke up to Annie's nose inches away from my nipple. She was definitely curious. And you can guess the next piece of this story: She wanted to breast-feed too—even though she had been weaned for a year. I was sure she had forgotten all about it. In desperation I called my local La Leche League volunteer, who assured me that this sort of behavior is natural. "Let her try it," she advised. "After drinking cow's milk for all this time, I don't think she'll like the taste."

Sure enough, she was right. Annie wouldn't even swallow. We both agreed that Mommy's milk was just for babies, not for big girls like her.

Even if you have prepared your older child to see you breast-feeding, it will still be a novelty of sorts. Luckily the newness soon wears off, and the whole event becomes commonplace. Then your challenge will be keeping your firstborn occupied while you nurse. (See chapter 8 for more on breast-feeding after the first week.)

Coping with Second-Baby Blues

During your first weeks home, you'll probably recognize the familiar "weepy" signs of baby blues. Not to be confused with postpartum depression (see chapter 8)—which is much more serious and can present itself anytime from the first month to the first year—baby blues presents itself a few days after you give birth. For a second-time mother, these feelings of anxiety and sadness often combine with guilt and a strong sense of feeling overwhelmed.

"One minute I'd be sitting in bed with both kids and feeling completely fulfilled: I had my family now and everything was right with the world," remembers Simone. "The next minute I'd be crying, thinking, *I'm ignoring my older child, I'm tired, I'm snubbing my husband, I'll never be able to do it all.*"

According to the American College of Obstetricians & Gynecologists, about seven out of every ten new mothers get the baby blues after childbirth. This statistic changes little with the birth of the second child, although the blues may seem rougher the second time around, since indeed, life is more overwhelming after the second child.

While these feelings seem powerful at the time, baby blues tend to last only a few hours at a time and usually go away after the first week or so. Your body is once again adjusting to the hormonal and emotional changes of having a baby. Recognizing baby blues as something temporary will help you pass through those days more easily.

What If the Baby Must Stay in the Hospital?

It can be extremely disappointing to your oldest to discover that after all the preparations—the sleeping arrangements, the homecoming outfit chosen—your baby can't come home right away. This happened to Molly and Sean, whose second baby had jaundice, a condition that kept him in the hospital for a week after Molly was discharged. Their four-year-old, Eddie, was very upset, and it wasn't until both parents sat down and explained as honestly as possible the reason for the delay that he calmed down. Molly's advice: "Assure your oldest that it's not his fault, that he's still going to be a big brother, and that he can help by drawing some pictures or sending photographs along to the hospital. Eddie wanted me to put his drawings in the bassinet under the fluorescent-type light so our baby could see them. I think he felt better knowing he had helped in some way."

There are many circumstances—some serious, some routine—that might keep your baby from coming home for days or even weeks. Although it will be difficult for you and your husband, it will be equally so for your older child, who's been anticipating the arrival of a new brother or sister. Your oldest will certainly be confused and upset, especially if the child senses that you're keeping the truth from him or her. Be clear and direct in your responses. Admit that you miss the baby too, but try to focus on the positive developments.

⇥ TIPS FROM THE TRENCHES ⇤

◆ My girlfriends—all mothers of two children or more—got together and hired a cleaning service to come the fourth day I was home. It was the best present I ever got—even though I was worried at the time it would be too disruptive. They came early in the morning and cleaned the whole house while I stayed in bed watching TV and nursing Benny and playing cards with Leo. They knocked on the door around noon, and the three of us moved downstairs to the den while they changed sheets, vacuumed, hung up clothes, and removed candy wrappers and yogurt containers from my bed stand. It was heaven!

—*Teresa, Boulder, Colorado*

◆ My husband brought home a baby doll for my five-year-old. It came with a bottle, and the doll "wet" herself. The first week my daughter and I bottle-fed our "babies" and changed their diapers together. It really helped her get over that hump of the first-week jealousy and kept her occupied but still close to me.

—*Rosie, Staten Island, New York*

◈ My husband slept in the guest room the first week, at my request. With our first child, I was obsessed with equality—both of us sharing baby care. I soon realized how ridiculous that was during the first week, when I nursed every two hours or so. This time my husband got to sleep so he could work the next day, and I could sleep with the baby if I wanted to.

—*Shelly, Melbourne, Florida*

8

The First Months

I had a little bit of the baby blues with my first baby, but full-fledged postpartum depression hit me at the end of the first month after my second was born. I became completely overwhelmed by the prospect of raising two children and obsessed over the idea that this was my fate for the next twenty years. I'd cry on and off all day, then be unable to sleep at night. I finally found treatment, but it was a hard journey.   *—Jana, Alexandria, Virginia*

As I look back now, those first few months with my baby and toddler were some of my happiest days ever. I sort of entered another world, staying in my pajamas and just playing with them both all day. I had had three miscarriages previously, and at age forty I couldn't believe God had actually given me two healthy children. I didn't care about the house or even my husband during that time—just the thrill that I finally had two!   *—Ruth, Glenview, Illinois*

I was so tired the first few months—before I was able to establish a routine of any kind—that I actually fell asleep once while on the phone. Both kids were napping and I had called my bank to move some funds. I was put on hold for a few minutes, and I just passed out—even with that horrible music playing in my ear!

—*Holly, Dearborn, Michigan*

For me, the first few months with two children were really the most challenging time. After the first week, my husband returned to work, and after the second week, my mother went back home to Wisconsin. Close friends continued to call, but less often. Neighbors and friends ended visits and phone calls with the same refrain: "Well, you're an old hand at this mothering stuff—by now it should be much easier!"

Nothing could have been further from the truth. I was now alone with two children during the day, and it seemed to me that everyone else had jumped ship. I would wait impatiently for my husband to come home at four o'clock each day. God help him if he was even ten minutes late. I'd be standing at the screen door with Alex in my arms and Annie at my feet and I'd sort of thrust both kids at him and say, "Now I can take a shower!" and race upstairs before he could say a word. During those early months much of each day seemed endless and unformed. Although postpartum depression never set in, I usually felt unequipped to handle the daily custodial care two very young children demanded. In short, life seemed so damned hard. "Why is it so hard with just one more?" I'd wonder to myself as I tripped over a toy or picked up a spilled cup of Cheerios or cranked up the baby swing or changed yet another diaper.

And yet, there were also good days—like the day Alex smiled his first smile—not at me, as I'd been trying for weeks—but at his sister, who jumped up and down with glee at the sight of his toothless gums. Or the day we went on our usual stroller walk and decided to go into a neighborhood church that was having a choral practice. In the dark vestibule, I squatted next to the stroller, and the three of us listened in awe as the choir sang out "Amazing Grace" a cappella. I will never forget the expression on Annie's and Alex's faces—eyes and mouths round as circles—as they listened. Even then, wearing sweatpants, spit-up on my shoulder, dopey with sleep deprivation, I knew that I was experiencing one of the magic moments of motherhood.

Someone—probably a mother of two young children—once said that having two children is really like having four children. Regardless of that illogical equation, two children is much more than double the work. The one constant in the first few months with your two children will be its daily unpredictability. In fact, the way your days unfold will be determined largely by the changing needs of your baby and your oldest.

My friend JoAnn remembers the early months of caring for her two as much easier than with her first. She attributes that to the fact that her second baby had such a different sleeping pattern. "She slept so much the first three months I thought she was deaf. I called the doctor in a panic, because I compared her with my first, who *never* slept through the night in two years!"

Another mother remembers that her two-year-old gave her more problems than her baby. "He had always taken an afternoon nap around one o'clock. But when I finally got the baby down for a nap at the same time, he would jump out of his bed and refuse to lie down. That used to drive me crazy! I wanted the solitude of that hour or so, and that was when my son wanted me all to himself."

Crystal recalls the highs and lows of the early months. "Some days were great," explains Crystal. "I'd take them both for a ride in the double stroller, we'd come home, they'd take a nap while I called my sister, we'd have dinner waiting for my husband. Other days were nightmares—neither would nap, the oldest would have a tantrum, the baby would be colicky. My husband used to phone me from the office before he left to come home just to get a read on what to expect that night."

Finding a Routine

With the first few weeks of chaos under your belt, you may begin to observe your children falling into vague patterns with regard to meals, naps, and bedtime. Ah, could it be that this could be the beginning of the magic word, "routine"? A daily routine can give a sense of order to second-time mothers while it soothes the psyche of both the oldest child and the baby. Granted, this routine will be ever-changing, since both baby and oldest will develop rapidly from month to month. Still, having a fluid, rough draft of a routine can make for easier sailing.

I found that after a month or so, my days were starting to take a kind of shape. I helped the process along a bit by blocking out my own time schedule, as listed below:

Get Up at the Same Time Each Day

I'd nurse Alex, then wake up Annie, even if she was sleeping. I know that a toddler sleeping means having time for yourself, but I found out that she developed better sleeping habits this way. If she got up while I was nursing, she'd either crawl into bed and watch, or my husband would make her breakfast and the two of them would chat in the kitchen.

Schedule Three Meals and Two Snacks Daily

Besides breakfast, lunch, and dinner, I'd present a late morning snack and a midafternoon snack, whether it was requested or not.

Snack time represented another fixed point in the day, and Annie learned to wait for her snack until then. Because I was nursing, it was a bit tricky and took a little thought.

Schedule Nap or Quiet Time

Besides a morning nap for Alex, both kids napped in the afternoon. This was my own downtime, and it became very precious to me. Annie often slept for an hour or so, and when that happened I actually got to read the paper, get my mail, and so on. I almost always spent nap time on my bed. Sometimes I just lay there, heart racing, as I contemplated the bizarre experience of being alone. Even on the days when Annie did not nap, she understood that the hour after lunch meant quiet time, and she lay in bed, looking at picture books or playing quietly—most of the time.

Take an Outing Each Day

I found that getting out for even a little bit each day was crucial to my sense of well-being. An outing could mean simply a stroller walk around the block, to my neighbor's house, or to the playground. Sometimes I dared to try more advanced outings, such as the grocery store or even a mall. Getting out in the late afternoon also gave us something to do during those "before dinner" hours when all of us tended to feel cranky.

Organize Dinner

I tried to set the table and have a general idea of what to cook—i.e., what to unthaw—by midafternoon. Upon returning from our outing I'd try to clear the dining area of toys and clutter so that there was a little oasis of order for my husband and me to experience once he came home. I'd nurse Alex while my husband fed

Annie and then—on good days—the adults managed a few minutes of dinner while Alex and Annie, confined to baby seat and high chair, watched cartoons nearby.

Have a Bath and Bed Ritual

My husband helped a great deal with this ritual, since we really needed one parent to pay attention to each child. By this time, all four of us were tired, so this became the hardest part of the day. Annie wanted both of us to put her to bed, like in the good old days, and most nights I was busy with Alex. We compromised by my coming into Annie's room and saying my "special good night" after her lights were out.

Yes, it was a long day, every day, but having a schedule—albeit a very rough schedule—gave me the sense of control that I needed. I still use the backbone of that schedule today with my family.

Breast-feeding and Bottle-feeding Strategies

Whether you are nursing or bottle-feeding your baby, mealtimes can be especially unnerving. No doubt you've discovered, like many mothers did, that the minute you sit down to feed your baby, your toddler or preschooler suddenly feels weak with hunger. To make matters worse, your oldest may now want to be spoon-fed animal crackers or insist that the juice be put in a bottle, although both these regressive acts tend to be only temporary. In addition, mealtimes can be especially hard to orchestrate because your baby may be nursing or bottle-feeding at two- or three-hour intervals. Here are some tips that can make feedings easier:

While You Are Breast-feeding

Have a snack ready for your oldest. Yogurt, juice, or cookies can be placed near the nursing area beforehand so that your oldest can be part of the feeding schedule.

Let your oldest choose a book or simple toy to bring to the nursing area. Agile moms can nurse and read a story or play a game at the same time. This takes practice, though; your oldest can help by holding the book or moving the game piece for Mom. Nursing on the floor with large pillows may make this an easier task.

If you're having trouble being calm enough for your milk to flow, try doing some of the relaxing breathing tips you learned in childbirth classes with your toddler. It will be a game for your child and may put you both in the right mood.

While You Are Bottle-feeding

Your oldest can bring a doll and "feed" it while you feed your newborn.

Let your oldest bring the bottle up to the baby's lips and tilt the bottle back. This can be a thrilling experience for a young child.

Occasionally, put your infant in the baby seat with a bottle so you can play with your oldest at this time.

Try to arrange at least one of the feedings for when your husband is home so that he can play one-on-one with your older child or bottle-feed the baby himself. Alternating these chores will enable your older one to spend individual time with both of you.

Many mothers try to feed the baby a morning meal early before the older child has awakened. This allows for special private bonding time for Mom and baby before the day begins. I remember nursing both kids as infants very early in the morning; I used to position myself in my rocking chair so that I could watch dawn rise. Despite my fatigue, I used to really enjoy those moments. And with Alex, that time became even more precious because once Annie was awake, my time was divided between them. By the same token, my private time with Annie came at the end of the day, after Alex had been nursed and put to sleep. I'd sit in Annie's "big girl" bed and read or just listen to her chatter on about her day. Those few minutes seemed to make the whole day end with a feeling of satisfaction.

Postpartum Depression with the Second Baby

The baby blues, which at least half of first- and second-time mothers develop, are an extremely common reaction occurring during the first week after delivery. Those symptoms—crying for no apparent reason, impatience, irritability, restlessness, and anxiety—come along sooner than with your first baby. Although unpleasant, they usually disappear on their own within a week or so.

Postpartum depression, however, is a serious condition that can last much longer and may present itself from the first month to the baby's second birthday.

According to the national nonprofit organization Depression After Delivery (DAD), founded in 1985 in order to provide support to women with postpostpartum depression, at least one in ten new mothers experience various degrees of postpartum depression. With the birth of the second child, those risk factors may increase. Symptoms include:

- sluggishness, fatigue, exhaustion
- sadness, depression, hopelessness

- appetite and sleep disturbances
- overconcern for the baby
- lack of interest in the day
- fear of harming the baby or yourself
- lack of interest in sex

Some mothers may not feel depressed, but they may experience acute anxiety, which is associated with panic disorder. Postpartum anxiety is characterized by:

- intense anxiety and/or fear
- rapid breathing
- fast heart rate
- sense of doom
- hot or cold flashes
- chest pain
- shaking or dizziness

Postpartum distress may include obsessive-compulsive features, called postpartum obsessive-compulsive disorder. If a mother has a history of OCD or if she showed signs of it during her first postpartum, these symptoms may intensify. They include: (1) intrusive, repetitive thoughts (including thoughts of harming the baby); (2) avoidance behavior (avoiding the baby to alleviate intrusive thoughts); and (3) extreme anxiety and depression.

The most severe form of postpartum distress is called postpartum psychosis, in which a woman experiences a break with reality. She may display hallucinations, delusions, and other bizarre feelings. Postpartum psychosis is a serious emergency and requires immediate medical help. Fortunately, it is the rarest postpartum reaction and occurs in about one in one thousand women, usually within the first month after the birth.

What Can You Expect This Time?

Dr. Susan Feingold is a past president of DAD and an Illinois clinical psychologist who specializes in women's hormonal disorders. A mother of two children, she first became interested in this field when she experienced postpartum depression after the birth of her second baby. "If you've had the normal baby blues with your first, you will definitely know the difference if you get postpartum depression with your second. It's a very debilitating experience. Symptoms generally get worse instead of just going away, as in baby blues."

Is there a higher risk with your second child? "What we've found is that if a woman had postpartum depression with her first child, then she has up to a 30 to 50 percent chance of contracting it again with her second," she explains. "However, if she did not have any symptoms with her first child, she may still contract PPD; the risk factors are slightly higher than with a first-time mother."

Are You at Risk This Time?

Simply the fact that you've had a second child may make you susceptible to PPD. "With a newborn and an older child, a mother's mood symptoms—anger, irritability, mood swings, losing control—may be much more intense simply because she's under so much more stress this time," warns Dr. Feingold. There are several additional factors that link the likelihood of PPD with second-time mothers. You are at risk if:

- You had PPD after your first child.
- Depression or anxiety runs in your immediate family.
- You have experienced severe and/or prolonged PMS, with its intense mood swings.

◆ You have just stopped breast-feeding or stopped taking the pill, and your hormones are irregular.

Getting Treatment

"In the past, women were reluctant to talk openly about their emotions with their obstetricians—and doctors were often ill-equipped to diagnose and treat PPD," states Dr. Feingold. "Women could suffer weeks before getting help." Fortunately, there's a greater awareness of PPD nowadays and the medical profession is on the lookout for the onset of its symptoms.

"Ideally, a woman who knows she's at risk for PPD should find a mental health professional before her second baby is born," states Dr. Feingold. "Together they can set up a postpartum plan of treatment. Often talk therapy is enough to treat mild forms of PPD. The patient and therapist concentrate on coping methods, such as getting help around the house, hiring a *doula*, and using a strong support network of other mothers."

There have also been advances using antidepressants to treat more severe PPD. Recent studies of Zoloft and Prozac, for example, show that these drugs do not interfere with the milk production in breast-feeding.

Fathers Can Help

"It's certainly easier to treat a woman for PPD if she has a sympathetic and supportive husband," say Dr. Feingold. "And fathers need support themselves at this time because they're really the family foundation during this difficult period. I will often ask the husband to come in for a session to talk about support strategies." Here are her suggestions for Dads:

• What you say can make a difference. In this case, platitudes do help: "You'll be okay"; "Don't worry, we'll get through this"; "I'll be there for you." Many women, fraught with guilt over their behavior, worry that their husbands will leave them.

• Never mention the condition of the house. Get someone to help with the household chores, or do the work yourself if necessary. A cleaning service can be hired once a week, once a month, or just once.

• Keep realistic expectations and encourage your wife to do the same. The baby may not be sleeping much, your toddler may have regressed to wearing diapers again, the laundry basket may be overflowing, and dinner may consist of Taco Bell take-out. It's your job to let your wife know that that's just fine, for right now.

• Spend as much time as possible with both children. Take the older child to the movies, to play video games, for a bike ride. Bring the baby over to your mother's for dinner. Take both kids for a ride to the car wash or to the library to give your wife some private time.

Making Space for Two

Your living space changed dramatically, as you may recall, with the birth of your first child. It's always amazing to see how much equipment a teeny tiny baby needs. Baby swing, playpen, baby seat, high chair, changing table, diaper bag, diaper pail, intercom, crib—the list is endless. As the baby grows, the child-proofing begins. Suddenly your glass cocktail table, ceramic objets d'art, electrical outlets, and even laundry chute become potential hazards. You install cabinet locks, place plastic gates at doorways, cover outlets, and block off stairways.

All this needs to be repeated after the arrival of your second baby, of course. But in addition, you need to make space for your firstborn too. Your baby may have spent the first few weeks in your bedroom—especially if you've been nursing—or just outside your room in order to be close for night feedings. But where will the newborn's permanent space be?

If you are lucky enough to have space big enough for both children to have their own room, you've just prevented a host of challenges. Each child will automatically have his or her own area to sleep and play in. However, if you are like many parents with less space, you will need to set up a shared room.

Your Firstborn's Reaction

Your child's world changes dramatically when he or she is forced to share space. Not only is there this new person that takes up all of Mom and Dad's time, but now this interloper must sleep in the same room! To further complicate matters, the child may not have the verbal skills as yet to articulate these anxieties. Even if you've prepared your child ahead of time, reassure the child that at least half of the room will remain "his or her place." Point out the area where your child can keep special toys and remind your child that he or she doesn't have to share them with the baby unless the child wants to. If your child is able to take an active role in the decision-making process—"Where shall we put the baby's crib?"—the child will be better able to handle the change.

Organizing a Room for Two

Stephanie Winston, best-selling author of *Best Organizing Tips* and *Getting Out from Under: A Personal Program for Change*, advises parents to think through the needs of both children before they begin to set up the room. "The idea is to organize the room to fit the children, not the other way around," says Winston. "For example, if the older child is allowed to stay up later than the baby, then he should have a light over his bed, so that he can read without disturbing the baby. He should have a place—not necessarily a separate closet, but a specific area—for his shoes. It is the first step in creating an orderly life," states Winston. "Even a two-year-old should learn that when she goes to bed at night she places her shoes in the same place." It is possible to arrange a room for two children in which each child has a sense of privacy and "territoriality." Here are Winston's tips for setting up a room for a baby and toddler:

- If the closet must be shared, paint the closet rod two different colors, so the oldest knows how far his or her territory goes.
- Line the room with low shelves, placing the very low shelves on the baby's side and the slightly higher shelves on the toddler side. Each toy should be laid out separately on the shelves.
- Put a tension rod up in the closet so it can be raised as the children get older.
- Use suction cup hooks on the back of the door, at different heights, so that the children can hang up their own shirts.
- Paint half the room one color, half another to mark private space.
- Use stackable plastic bins for the children's toys. A toy chest, while a romantic concept, generally makes kids plow through to the bottom to get a toy, disrupting the other stuff on top.
- Reserve a corner of the room for play-in-progress—a Lego project, a puzzle, a board game.
- Every six months, rethink your growing children's needs. Pack up unused toys, redistribute the plastic bins, raise hooks.

Winston also believes that teaching very young children—even toddlers—a sense of order is one of the most important gifts a parent can give a child. "Kids become disturbed if their eyes cannot settle or focus on one thing. Confusion and chaos breed anxiety," she states. "And the bonus is that an orderly bedroom can make life so much easier for Mom. The more orderly both children are, the smoother the house is run and the less overwhelmed the whole family is."

The "Advanced" Outing: Have Courage!

Sooner or later you will have to take your children on your own errands. Trips to the supermarket, the library, the mall, and the doctor's office all require a great deal of preparation. However long it took you to go out with one child, count on leaving more than twice the time to manage two.

I will never forget my first grocery store trip with both kids. At the time, Annie was almost two years old and Alex was two months old. The only outing up until then had been an occasional stroller walk around the block. I was well aware how important it is to expose young children to outside stimuli and was determined to master a trip to the grocery store. After all, I had done it with one child. How hard could two be?

Here's a basic rundown:

1. Prepare the children. Change the baby's diaper. Dress the baby. Put a jacket on the baby. Put the baby in the baby seat. Buckle the strap. Put a pacifier in his mouth. Pick up the pacifier. Wash it. Put it back in his mouth.

2. Put the toddler in the playpen. Go outside and strap in the baby's car seat. Go inside, take the toddler out of the playpen.

Put a jacket on the toddler. Zip the jacket. Tie her shoes. Wipe her nose. Try to scrape crystallized Fruit Loops from her jacket lapel.

3. Put on a clean sweatshirt. Brush teeth. Put my hair in *Shogun*-style ponytail without bothering to comb. Grab the diaper bag, a plastic bag of healthy snack food, the grocery coupons, my purse, the keys.

4. Hold the infant seat containing the baby in one hand, clutch the toddler's arm with the other. Carry my purse in my teeth.

5. Open the front door. Sniff. Return to the playroom. Place the toddler in playpen.

6. Unstrap the baby from the infant seat. Carry him to the changing table. Carry him to the front door where the diaper bag is. Take a diaper out of the diaper bag. Bring the diaper to the changing table while still carrying the baby, but first swing by the playpen to insert Zweiback into screaming toddler's mouth. Change the diaper.

7. Return to the front door with both kids. Make it to the car. Set infant seat down on driveway, catching it as it lists to the right. Steady it with my left foot while opening back door. Lift toddler into her cat seat, contorting my own body to strap toddler in while holding the infant seat up with my left foot.

8. Lift the infant seat into the backseat and strap it in while the toddler shoves a headless Gumby into the baby's ear.

9. Place a large pillow between car seat and infant seat.

10. Get into the front seat. Strap on the seat belt. Take a deep breath. Put *Janis Joplin's Greatest Hits* into the cassette player. Blast. Drive.

This is not an exaggeration, as many of you know. Once inside the grocery store, both children, instinctively sensing a chance for real drama—and with an audience!—responded loudly to the colors and noise of a large supermarket. With the baby unaccustomed to a new, attached, shopping-cart baby seat and my oldest huddled on the floor of the cart, sandwiched in between the frozen Weight Watchers dinners and the canned ham, neither was a happy camper. The whining began in stereo. They were so *loud*. I, mortified by other shoppers' glares, tried to compensate by "speed shopping"—racing up and down the aisle, grabbing cereal on the right, disposable diapers on the left. My toddler began to imitate me, one arm leveling the tampon display, the other swatting down salad dressing.

By the time we were waiting on the cashier's line, I was rigid with embarrassment. Ripping open a nearby bag of Cheetos, I placed two in my toddler's hands. They were a welcome relief from the nasty carrots and she chomped appreciatively and became quiet. At that moment, I remember thinking this was payback for all the times I had watched mothers giving their kids high-fat, sugary junk food and thought, "When I have children, I will only allow nutritious snacks." Ha.

Experience is a great educator. I now realize, too, in our first foray out into civilization, that I was overly sensitive to the children's noise level. People in supermarkets, in malls, in children's libraries are used to children. Two normal children do make a commotion wherever they go, and I've become almost militant in support of parents' right to be seen with their children in public. My feeling is this: If society wishes to continue reproducing the human species, it will just have to put up with a little noise.

Dad and the Two Kids

Although times are changing and much has been written about fathers taking on a greater role in child-caring chores, most mothers are quick to point out that the division of labor remains somewhat lopsided. Mothers still tend to take on most of the child-care chores when a couple has their first child. But after the second baby, fathers are generally pressed into duty out of sheer need. In fact, a big plus to having a second child is that it increases the father's involvement in his family.

"We began dividing up the chores after the first month," says Steve. "I saw that with two, there was no choice. So I started getting Brian up and ready for preschool while my wife fed Adriana. At the end of the day it was I who gave him a bath and read him a story. I also started doing a lot of the grocery shopping on my way home from work."

George saw a big change in the division of chores after their second son was born. "I am doing a whole lot more of the custodial care than I ever did with our firstborn," he admits. "In fact, it's only now that I realize how much work my wife did—pretty much alone—with our first."

Sharing Child Care and Household Chores

Determining who is going to do what is one of the most difficult issues that parents of young children face. With two children to care for, each parent will think he or she is the one doing most of the work. That's because each child needs so much attention. Add to that the endless household chores that need to be shared. When husbands take part in both kinds of chores, it not only helps their wives, but it also helps the marriage. But it's important that fathers share in the child-care chores for other reasons too. A young child gains a sense of security and belonging when both Mom *and* Dad are taking an active role in raising him or her. The child grows up with a stronger sense of equality between the sexes when the child sees a balance in the job roles at home. And studies have shown that fathers can be just as sensitive, nurturing, and attuned to a baby's behavior as mothers.

As true as these sentiments are, it's not always easy to get your husband to help—or even to notice that you need help in certain areas. That's where communication comes in. Psychologists and family therapists agree that to get help, you must ask for it. It sounds simple, but many of us sabotage ourselves with vague, muttered complaints instead of workable solutions. The division of child care is ultimately a power negotiation, and the act of sharing works best when both parties agree on the terms. Here are some ways to divide child care and household chores:

Be Specific About Your Needs. Whining about how tired you are and making vague complaints such as "I just can't do it all alone" and "How can you just sit there and watch TV while I'm killing myself?" will only make your husband want to escape. Instead, sit down together and list the chores. Make it clear that you sympathize with the fact that he is working at an outside job. Ask him what he feels comfortable doing. Try to agree on a few specific chores, such as getting the older child up and dressed and serving breakfast.

Don't Criticize the Job He Is Doing. Bite your tongue when you see that the laundry has been washed and dried, but has funny pink streaks in the whites. So what if the cups are stacked wrong in the dishwasher? If he bought the wrong size diapers, don't mention it; he'll figure it out the next time he changes a diaper.

Praise, Praise, Praise. Swoon over his microwaved dinners. Weep over his recycling skills. Remind him at the end of the day how much you appreciated it when he took both kids for a ride in the car for an hour.

Remember that the more fathers participate in the family network, the more involved they become in their children's daily lives. The relationship between husband and wife can blossom when both are working together toward the common good.

Your Sex Life . . . Remember?

Speaking of the common good, returning to a sex life with your husband can be an important element in reviving your relationship. Most women generally wait three to six weeks—less if they have not had an episiotomy—to resume sexual relations. After a cesarean, your doctor will probably advise that you wait at least six weeks. Even when you are physically able to resume sex, you may not be ready emotionally.

It is hard enough to go back to being romantic after having one child. But with two, most women—and some men—are simply too exhausted to even think about sex for the time being. The constant negotiations about the child-care chores can cause resentment that may transfer into less interest in sex for either or both parties. For women, there is the added trauma of (even more) physical changes to the body and the hormonal changes they undergo with childbirth and breast-feeding.

"My husband and I used to go to it like rabbits," admits Rachel. "After our first was born, it slowed down a little, but we still got together during Seth's Saturday afternoon naps. But since Nell was born, we're lucky if we have an hour a week to spare for ourselves. And if we do, most of the time we'd rather just sleep!"

Despite relentlessly cheerful articles in women's magazines— "Fabulous Sex After Triplets!"—the truth is that most couples agree that their sex life temporarily disappears after the birth of the second child. It takes weeks—sometimes months—to get back into the swing of things romantically. Many couples find that setting aside specific time each week for each other helps.

"We have a standing date every Friday night," explains Clarissa. "A sitter comes at six, and I meet my husband at a local restaurant after he finishes work. That way we've separated ourselves from the household chores and, for a while at least, we're a couple." Clarissa goes on to say that when they shift roles from parents to a couple, they're more likely to continue that role in bed together later.

⇥ TIPS FROM THE TRENCHES ⇤

◆ Get out of the house at least once a day with your kids. If I stayed in more than two days in a row, the kids became impossible and I got really cranky. A trip to the mall or even just to your next-door neighbor's house keeps everything in perspective those first few months. —*Bette, Syosset, New York*

◆ I didn't breast-feed with my first—I had trouble with sore breasts and insufficient milk supply, and I just gave up. But I did success in nursing my second baby. I was so worried that my three-year-old would be jealous, but he was fine with it. In fact, he hardly even noticed. I'm so glad I tried again. It's really worth it. —*Margie, New York, New York*

◆ The best thing I ever did was to hire our neighbor's eleven-year-old as a mother's helper for two hours each afternoon. Sometimes she played with my oldest, sometimes she folded laundry, sometimes she changed diapers. I was always in the house, but I could make phone calls and stay upstairs and relax a little. —*JoEllyn, Great Neck, New York*

9

The First Year . . .
and Beyond

When It Hit Me:
We're a Family of Four

Going to a restaurant and the hostess asking, "How many?" Our six-year-old piped up, "A family of four, please." My husband and I exchanged glances; he laughed and all of a sudden, I got choked up.   —*Melanie, Sacramento, California*

During Mass, when the usher asked us to "present the Eucharistic gifts." All four of us walked up the aisle carrying the host and the wine while the deacon announced each of our names.   —*Debbie, Baltimore, Maryland*

When we had a professional photograph taken of the four of us for a Christmas photo card. I couldn't stop staring at the photo. There we were! I was holding our fourteen-month-old, and our five-year-old was sitting between my husband and me. Suddenly I realized we were an official family.   —*Monica Jo, Detroit, Michigan*

I remember thinking we had gone over the hump of infancy to actual childhood—or at least toddlerhood—when Alex celebrated his one-year birthday with a "party" of three other one-year-olds. Annie, at two and a half, looked so big in contrast to her brother. She acted terribly important too, and wanted to help—by blowing out Alex's candles, opening up Alex's gifts, and disciplining Alex's playmates. "No, no, no!" she hollered at a boy who had barely touched a piece of wrapping paper.

Throughout the past year I had watched Annie interact with her brother. Sometimes she was jealous, sometimes she was bored, and sometimes she was angry, but on this day I watched her turn into the "older sister." It was a characteristic that would continue on far past toddlerhood. Alex, on the other hand, had until now been the designated "baby." I saw now that he was turning into a full-fledged member of our family. I felt a momentary twinge of sadness, knowing that he was my last baby. I knew with each developmental milestone that I was letting go of a moment that I could never recapture.

That day, as my husband and I sang happy birthday and passed slices of cake to the parents and children, it seemed that we had settled into a family of four. There was no doubt that we were still in the thick of it all—parenting meant long hard hours, and the constant custodial care of our children—but the earlier zombie days and nights had shifted into a manageable routine, and the four of us were adjusting to each other's personalities. We were also watching other families settle in. On our street there are four families of four, and over the years we've all watched the children, not only grow up and develop, but also interact with each other as they go through friendships and stages of development with each other. Most interesting to observe are the always-changing relationships of the siblings.

The Growing Relationship Between Your Children

As your baby becomes an active, mobile toddler and your older child continues to mature in that first year, the family dynamics change too. The different ages, the age spacing, the birth order, and the sex of each child all play a part in the evolution of their relationship After the first year, each child's personality becomes more finite and unique. Your oldest, who may have regarded the baby as a minor—or major—inconvenience, may now view the baby in a different way. Your oldest may note, for example, that the baby is turning into a *person*.

My daughter first took notice of Alex's new maturity on the day that she threw some stuffed animal into the playpen and Alex responded with a quite clear and emphatic "No" and threw the toy right back at Annie. Annie's eyes grew wide with shock. She stood up and threw it back in the playpen. Alex threw it back at her, and *voila*, they had just had their first sibling fight.

Coping with Sibling Battles

As your children age, the potential for trouble between them increases. As thrilling as it is to observe your two children playing together, it is disheartening to watch them quarrel. This is especially hard when our expectations are that siblings should automatically love each other. If we, as children, longed for a close sibling relationship—a confidante, a pal—then the pain of witnessing our children fighting is even worse. My husband, for example, was an only child, and when he sees our children bickering over a toy or arguing over the remote control, he is horrified at their behavior. "What's wrong with them?" he asks. "They shouldn't be fighting like that!"

Yet experts tell us that sibling fights are quite normal and even healthy. In fact, the way each child battles and struggles over ownership of toys and the attention of parents teaches coping and negotiation skills. However, for a parent trapped in the same room with two quarreling toddlers, it is a less than pleasant experience.

Nothing is more nerve-racking and exhausting than having to endure your two children fighting. Jane Nelson, Ed.D., author of several parenting books including *Positive Discipline for Preschoolers*, and a nationally known education specialist, has spent a career teaching discipline techniques to parents. "Before you try to change a child's behavior, it's important to understand his belief system," she says. "His behavior is just a code for the belief system. If a toddler watches his mother coo over the new baby, the toddler may go over to the baby when his mother is not watching and hit the baby over the head. The behavior is not acceptable, of course, but it may be the toddler's *belief system* that he is not loved anymore, or that his mother loves the baby more."

It is often difficult for a parent to convey an abstract concept like "equal love" to a young child. Nelson uses the following story to help second-time parents teach this concept in a more concrete fashion to children as young as three years old:

"Show four candles to your older child. Light the first candle and say, "This is an example of Mommy all by herself, and the fire is the love she has. Then Mommy marries Daddy, and she gives him her love." Now light the second candle. Point to the first candle. 'See how she still has love for herself?' Then light the third candle. 'Then you were born, and Mommy gave her love to you, but see how it didn't take away from the love of herself or Daddy?' Then light the fourth candle. 'Then your brother was born, and Mommy gave her love to him, but see how it didn't take away any love from you? All four candles are burning bright. That's the magic of love. It can grow and grow.'"

Even when children understand they are loved, there will still be times when they feel that Mom or Dad is playing favorites or is not being fair, and so instigate a fight. "It's helpful to see sibling fighting for what it usually is—just as puppies roll around together and investigate their roles, so do children. Often kids will fight simply to get the attention of the parent," explains Nelson. "Parents usually rush in and rescue the younger sibling, because they think he is being taken advantage of." Unless the younger one is in physical danger, Nelson advises a hands-off approach.

"Rescuing one child is making a statement to both. It says, 'You're the victim here; you can't take care of yourself. You need help.' Parents can avoid the rescuer role by staying out of sibling disagreements. By letting your children fend for themselves," Nelson states, "you are teaching both children important social skills."

It's not always easy listen to battling children, and Nelson asks parents to keep in mind her "three Bs" as options for coping with sibling fights.

The Three Bs

Option 1: Beat it. You leave the area. For parents of toddlers and preschoolers, for example, that may mean just walking out of the playroom into the kitchen, where you can still supervise, but from a distance. Children tend to stop fighting once they can't get a parent's attention. In fact, don't be surprised if they follow you. If you choose this method it's a good idea to tell them in advance that this is what you will do when they fight.

Option 2: Bear it. This is your hardest option, because it means staying in the room with the fighters, without jumping in to stop the fighting or to fix the problem. I use this option only when I am forced to, such as when I'm in the car. As Nelson suggests, I pull over to the side of the road and announce that I'll continue on the way to, say, Taco Bell, when the fighting stops.

Option 3: Boot 'em out. You send both kids away to separate spaces (like their bedrooms) to cool off. Or you can send them both outside if they want to continue the fight. They can decide to end the fight and stay on the premises—and continue watching TV, for example. I find sending each child to a separate room very helpful, as long as I can control my urge to lecture them on their bad behavior.

Lectures Don't Work

"Lectures are useless—and demeaning," explains Nelson. "It is far more respectful to ask the child how he thinks a problem can be solved. Even a three-year-old can contribute input. This teaches him to learn problem-solving skills. In our house there was a problem over chores. Each child thought his chores—whether it was emptying the garbage or feeding the cat—were harder than his sibling's. I didn't really know how to make chores completely 'equal,' but my son came up with the solution. He suggested I post all the necessary chores on the refrigerator door, and make each chore on a first come, first served basis. My daughter agreed with the idea, adding that a brief description of each chore be included. It worked—mainly because the idea came from them, not me."

"That's Not Fair!"

Although most of us try to be fair to both children, we soon find out that total fairness is impossible. Children are quick to point out that things are not equal in a household with different-aged children. My daughter stopped using the car seat after age five. My son, at three, was enraged that he still had to sit in his car seat. "It's not fair!" he screamed. "It's not fair," I think, was his first declarative sentence. All the explaining about federal age regulations concerning car seats did no good in his eyes.

Rather than being equal about privileges and punishments, I try to be age appropriate in those areas and treat them according to their needs. However, there are some areas where it pays to be absolutely, positively equal. I use my neighbor's trick when serving birthday cake: one child cuts the cake and the other child chooses the piece. It makes for great incentive to cut evenly, and it takes the pressure off the parent. However, when I'm forced to divvy up three cookies or other treats, I have no choice but to use a scalpel, if necessary, to cut the third cookie in equal parts.

Presenting a United Front

It is only natural for you and your mate to disagree at times about discipline methods. After all, you both came from different families and had different upbringings. Now that there are two children—often fighting themselves—it is critical that you come to terms with each other's philosophies.

Avoid arguing in front of the children, especially about discipline. They'll quickly interpret that as one parent taking their side and the other one not. And worse, children won't respect parents who show no respect for each other. If you walk into an ongoing situation and you disagree with your husband's methods, try not to interfere. Wait until you are both alone, and then discuss what happened.

You both need to be consistent in basic household rules and how to handle it when those rules are broken. If kids sense that parents don't agree, they will use one parent against the other. I found out recently, for example, that my son had been going to my husband, who's a real soft touch in the discipline department, to ask if he could watch *South Park* on television—after he had asked me first and gotten a resounding no.

The Reasons for Sibling Rivalry

Each one of us—adult and child—wants to be appreciated as a separate, unique human being. Being one of two children means a constant struggle for "uniqueness," for parental attention, for praise and closeness and intimacy. While we all try to encourage sharing, we also know deep down that it goes against nature. If you share your toys with your sister, you won't have as many to play with. It is natural for children to compete with one another. Competition can be a healthy and solid success skill when not overdone. If parents respect and support each other's differences, the children learn that behavior themselves.

Working Parents

For many parents these days, a two-income family is a necessity. In fact, according to the American Academy of Pediatrics, about 70 percent of parents have their children in some form of child care. You may have been working before the birth of your first child and stayed home through the first year after your second, or you may be returning to work for the second time. Regardless, many mothers returning to work after a second baby find this an extremely stressful period. Once she goes back to work she finds the demands of two children, a job, and keeping the household running almost intolerable.

In *The Second Shift*, a book that addresses the working mother's "second shift" of parenting every evening, author Arlie Hochschild writes that although having a baby is difficult for working parents, it is after the birth of their second child that their problems can reach crisis proportions.

"When I realized I was squeezing Desonex onto my toothbrush instead of toothpaste on Monday mornings, I knew I was stressed," admits my friend Kathy. "My returning to work was much harder the second time around."

Child Care for Two

Even if you've been through this process once before, a second child will present new challenges in the search for child care. You now need care for two children—each at a different developmental stage.

Choosing the right kind of care means taking the time to think over what child-care situation is the best for your children and the most practical for you. Caregivers can be family members, close friends, or licensed day care workers. The three basic choices you have are:

A Caregiver Who Comes to Your Home. This is the most convenient and can be the most comforting to both children and parents. Your children do not have to adjust to a new setting. There's certainly less trauma and separation anxiety for children kept in their own familiar surroundings. It gives you greater control over their environment. Home care may lessen your children's exposure to seasonal illnesses because they are less exposed to other kids.

This is also the most expensive way to go. It may be hard to find a skilled in-home provider who has her own transportation. This choice also requires a backup person, in the event that the caregiver is sick or goes on vacation. Since it's difficult to judge what exactly goes on in your absence, it is crucial to check out references. And finally, since your children will be home all day, you may come back to a house that looks like a cyclone hit it.

This was my choice for child care when I went back to work. I had our evening sitter's mother come in each morning and stay with Annie and Alex until I returned home at three o'clock. I was lucky because Kate's mother lived around the corner and was extremely reliable. It made mornings a little less hectic to know that neither my husband nor I would have to get the kids in the car and drive them to another home or day care facility. Although some moms arrange for the caregiver to also do light housework, I preferred constant attention for my two, who were at the extremely active ages of ten months and two-and-a-half years.

Child Care in the Home of the Caregiver. Many child-care providers who offer child care in their home have young children of their own, and they may care for other children the same ages. This can be beneficial to toddlers and preschoolers who enjoy playing together. However, since many family child-care providers usually work alone, it's hard to judge their work. Look for those who are licensed or registered with the state and therefore inspected. At the very least you should have high recommendations from other parents whose judgment you trust. Be sure to check out the home carefully when you visit. Are there separate areas for napping? Television should be limited to a couple of hours, not be blaring from morning to night. Six children should be the limit in a home. Since there is usually only one adult, ask about backup care in an emergency situation.

"This was the right solution for me," states Mary Margaret, a sales representative who commuted by train from the suburbs to New York City each day. "I dropped my eighteen-month-old and three-year-old at a home where the caregiver had two kids about the same ages as mine. My kids were ready for someone to play with. They looked forward to going there most days. She had been doing this sort of work for a couple of years, and my sister-in-law had used her services too. In the evening my husband picked them up whenever I had to work late or missed a train."

Center-Based Care in a Facility Designed for Young Children. These facilities fall under the names of preschool, nursery school, or leaning center. They can also have different sponsors, including churches, schools, colleges, and even corporate employees. Day care centers should be licensed and inspected regularly for health, safety, cleanliness, and staffing. Look for age-appropriate toys, a daily schedule, and the interaction of the staff with the youngsters.

Pat works at a company that has its own day care center onsite. "The truth is, that's why I stay at this job. The day care is so convenient. I just bring my kids to the center, then go into my office. I stop by at lunchtime and again in the afternoon. When I was still nursing I was able to take breast-feeding breaks at the center, then return to work. I won't start looking for another job until both kids are in kindergarten."

Whatever type of care you choose, look for the adult-to-child ratio. The American Academy of Pediatrics has formed the following chart to list recommended level of child-to-staff ratio, depending on the child's age.

AGE	CHILD:STAFF RATIO	MAXIMUM GROUP SIZE
Birth to 24 months	3:1	6
25 to 30 months	4:1	8
31 to 35 months	5:1	10
3-year-olds	7:1	14
4- and 5-year-olds	8:1	16
6- to 8-year-olds	10:1	20
9- to 12-year-olds	12:1	24

You'll want to consider the needs of each child in terms of his or her age and stage of development. A baby, for example, needs constant and consistent care and has his or her own individual needs for sleep, feeding, and play. Toddlers also need consistent and attentive care, but they also require someone who understands their need to explore and experiment with their environment. Experts agree that children age three and older benefit from being with other children their age. And a preschooler will not be able to thrive in an environment that is too boring or confining. Older children need even more diverse surroundings and can benefit from after-school programs and summer camps.

Does this mean you have to find two different child-care situations for your two kids? Some parents do, especially if their children are more widely spaced. "I had someone come to our home to care for our one-year-old," says one mother. "But our four-year-old needed some outside stimulation, so we brought her to a preschool center three mornings a week."

Considering your own practical needs is also important. "I was not about to stop at two different places to pick up both kids after working all day," says Amanda, a nurse practitioner. "I would have been too exhausted and would have ended up taking it out on the kids. Besides, it would have been cruel to separate them from me *and* from each other! So at age thirteen months and three, both boys went to a highly recommended day care center located on the way to the hospital."

Whatever type of child care you choose, the AAP offers these additional factors to consider:

- Quality of the adult/child relationships: Are the staff members trained in child development?
- Location: Can parents get there in an emergency?
- Hours: What happens if you are late in picking up your child?

- Alternative arrangements: What happens if your child is sick? Is there medical care available to the program?
- Consistency: Are the programs or caregiver's policies on meals, discipline, and toilet training the same as yours?

Finding Time

Ask any mother of two children what she needs most and the answer will be the same: more time. There never seems to be enough of it. The biggest obstacle is finding time for each child, time for your husband, time for yourself. You and your husband's busy schedules may make you feel as though you're racing through your days without being able to enjoy your children. If you're feeling frustrated, it's likely that your children are too. After all, they would rather spend time with their parents than anyone else. So how do you carve out time for them? Read how several ingenious mothers found creative ways to use precious pockets of time with their children:

> I'm in the car with both kids so much I started using it as a place for quality conversation. I turned off the radio. I stock the side pockets with snacks, pencils, drawing paper, and children's audio cassettes. Sometimes we sing along to *Sesame Street*, and sometimes my older son and I talk over a problem he may have had at recess that day. I've even helped my kids write thank-you notes in the car!
>
> —*Vivian, mother of a two- and five-year-old*

> I use the phone to keep in touch with the kids during the day. I call them as soon as I get to the office, and I call again as soon as I know they're both home from preschool. Around five, before I leave, I call again. I try to spend *exactly*

the same amount of time with each child—even though it's not easy having a five-minute conversation with a toddler!

—*Lianna, mother of two- and three-year-old*

I get up one hour before the rest of the family. I sit with my coffee and figure out my day. By the time the kids wake up, I'm completely dressed and have breakfast on the table. Then I can spend calm, relaxed time with them until our baby-sitter comes. *Julian, mother of a two- and four-year-old*

Making Time for Each Other

While most of us find it extremely challenging to be a good parent, we also have to admit that it's even harder to be a good spouse. It certainly takes the same patience, understanding, and most of all, effort to keep a relationship afloat as it does to be good parents. The demands of two growing children make it even more difficult to stay a couple.

If you think your life as a couple could use some improvement, take the time to talk about it. Communication can work wonders, and the two of you can find ways to make your lives together more satisfying.

"Once we talked about it, we figured out ways to lower our 'home stress' by getting out of the house more," states Jenny. "We started taking family walks around the block after dinner—Brian rode his two-wheeler and we pushed his brother in the stroller. That activity gave my husband and I a chance to just go over the day."

Setting aside one night a week for a date can also help. When you book your sitter, make it a standing weekly appointment. In fact, I wish I had put one of our teenage sitters on "retainer" for one night a week. That's what my friend Carol did, and she said it saved her marriage and her sanity.

"My husband works ten-hour days as an investment banker," explains Carol. "In addition, he is at the computer first thing every Saturday and Sunday morning. Between the kids and the computer, the only chance for us to have an actual conversation is when the baby-sitter comes. We know the meter is running, so to speak, and that gets us out of the house. Once we're out, we can focus on each other."

If that sounds too expensive, try this: Use a trade-off system with a friend in which you watch each other's youngsters. We were able to do that one year: On Friday afternoons we took turns with the couple across the street. It worked out fine, especially on the nights when it was our turn to have free time!

Another idea is to go away overnight once in a while if possible. "My husband was the one who suggested that we go to a Broadway show in New York City and stay overnight on our anniversary," remembers Cari. "I thought it was too expensive, I was too exhausted, and I was worried about leaving the kids with his parents. But he insisted, and boy, am I glad he did! Now we get away a few times a year, and it's really put the sizzle back in our relationship."

Creating a Strong Family

All families are different, but every family strives for a happy, secure, rewarding life. Yet families today are finding themselves crushed with high-pressure jobs, scheduled play dates, mountains of homework, long commutes, and myriad other pressures that threaten the nuclear family. How does a family stay afloat—remain close-knit and loyal in the swirling outside world? Much has been written on the subject, but the strong families I've observed and interviewed all seem to possess the same basis elements that keep them close and unified.

Family Meetings

Jane Nelson calls family meetings the single most important tradition for a well-run family. "Regular family meetings—complete with an agenda contributed by all family members—teach kids important life skills that will help them be successful in school, in business, and in marriage," she believes. "It teaches brainstorming, problem solving, and negotiating skills. It helps with discipline, because even in the middle of a sibling quarrel, the children can stop and put it on the agenda, and they'll know the problem will be addressed at Sunday's meeting."

Some guidelines for family meetings:

♦ The agenda should be a list of any family issues. A mother may write down: "Backpacks are being left on the kitchen table." A sibling may note: "I don't get to watch my favorite programs on Wednesday because my brother hogs the TV control." A father might write: "After church next week: mall or museum?" When a problem arises, write it on the agenda and make the agenda visible for all to see during the week.

♦ Make the meetings a part of the weekly routine—same time, same place. Sunday evenings work well for many families. The dining room table suggests a seriousness of purpose.

♦ Start each meeting with a compliment for each member of the family. At our family meetings, it was hard to get Annie and Alex to say something nice about each other without adding a "but," as in: "Alex loaned me his Nintendo 64, but I had to give it back right away." The compliment should be free of any additional qualifiers.

♦ The meeting should not take place during a meal. It should stand on its own, without distractions, making it an important event.

- End the meeting by planning a fun family activity for the coming week. Serve dessert or play a game together to close the meeting.

We've been holding family meetings for several years now, and they have really decreased sibling fights. Last summer when we had an extension put on our house, things grew hectic and for a while we stopped holding the meetings. Within a week the children began bickering, and their fights soon escalated to full-fledged battles. Now that we're back to weekly meetings, life has become calmer. My husband and I have found that the more we involve our kids in problem solving, the more confidence we have in their skills. I especially like the meetings because it makes me feel that despite our crazy time schedule, we are really a family rather than four people just rooming together.

Family Dinners

Our neighbors Carolyn and Seb managed to raise two well-mannered, enthusiastic, happy, loving daughters, who are now both in college. When I asked them what kept their family so close, they looked at each other and said in unison, "Family dinners." Carolyn and Seb made sure that the four of them sat down most nights for dinner. "It wasn't always a fancy dinner—sometimes it was just pizza or Chinese take-out. But we turned off the phone and actually talked," says Carolyn. Seb added that family dinners seemed natural because they started them when both girls were still in high chairs. "Of course, our dinners back then consisted of ten minutes of noisy chaos with one or two minutes of peace, but things improved over the years."

We all know why family dinners are important, but figuring out how to do them takes some effort. With family schedules so jam packed, it's hard to schedule a dinner when all four of you will be together. We've been setting aside Mondays, Thursdays, and Sundays for family dinners for some time. Be patient the first few times you eat together. It is usually *less* than relaxing at first. When children are young, just their presence at the table is a triumph. As they grow, they will become accustomed to the routine of washing their hands, helping to set the table, and enjoying a family conversation. Turning on restful music can set the mood. Try to make dinners a pleasant experience by asking about each child's day. Avoid criticism. Don't fight with your spouse—the children will pick up on the vibes. And although table manners are important, try not to make a big deal about them at first. Teach basic courtesy for starters, such as waiting until the whole family is seated before eating, asking to be excused, and so on. Make the dinners brief with small children; remember that they can sit still for only so long.

Family Chores

Giving children responsibility for certain chores will make them feel part of a larger group. Although it's true that teaching chores to toddlers takes more time than doing the chore yourself, it's important to teach your youngsters to help around the house at an early age.

According to Atlanta psychologist Elizabeth Ellis, a great number of children brought to her for counseling have never been given the opportunity to learn a sense of responsibility, which she defines as being able to meet the goals you've set and use problem-solving skills. Such children tend to be dependent on their parents to make decisions for them and have low self-esteem and poor coping skills when faced with everyday stress. "In Third World countries," Ellis observes, "a child of four is given a spoon and told to stir the pot because the parents are too busy doing other chores. As a result, those children often have high self-esteem—they know they are helping the family."

In this country of microwaves and take-out, we no longer need to have our children "stir the pot," but we still need to let them know they are a part of the family. Even very young children can take part in chores. Two- and three-year-olds can be taught to turn off lights when leaving a room and to put spoons in the dishwasher and dirty diapers in the pail. Four- and five-year-olds should be able to wash and dry their hands, dress themselves, refill a pet's water dish, get mail from the mailbox, make their beds, and pick out too-small clothes for Goodwill. By the time children reach ages six and seven, they can weed a garden, clean the bathroom sink, set the alarm clock, put dirty clothes in the hamper (separating the colors too), and address their own birthday party invitations.

Be sure to praise their efforts, and, most important, be consistent in your expectations. They will need reminding and encouragement, but the rewards of being a contributing member of the family will, in the end, outweigh the occasional complaint.

Family Traditions

Creating your own traditions is such an important part of developing a strong family that best-selling parenting authors Linda and Richard Eyre list it as one of three core principals in their book, *Three Steps to a Strong Family*. In it they write: "The reason to work at family traditions is that they offer opportunities to create memories, share love, and build strong bonds between family members. They will not only help your family life be more peaceful and rewarding, they will also give your children memories they can draw on no matter where they go or who they grow up to be."

If you look back on your own childhood, some of your happiest memories probably center around traditions—whatever your family did to celebrate or mark certain events. We want to create the same warm moments for our own family, or, if we don't have good childhood memories, we want to create traditions to be sure the same void isn't felt by our own children.

Family traditions don't need to be expensive or complicated productions. For example, when I was growing up, one of our holiday traditions was going to Christmas Eve mass and then riding around the neighborhood to look at Christmas decorations. I still remember sitting in the backseat of our Chevy Impala with my sister next to me as we oohed and ahhed at the colored lights. It is a tradition I've carried over with my own children, and each year they look forward to the consistency—and just plain fun—of our Christmas Eve ride.

Family vacations are natural tradition makers. Just getting away together—away from household chores and the hectic pace of daily life—can be refreshing. Whether we only go away for a few days or for a major trip like Disney World, we take part in several rites: The first night, wherever we are, we order room service. It may not sound significant enough to make it a "family tradition," but it's a big thrill for all of us to order from the room-service menu. The four of us sit around the television and decompress from our travels. Another vacation tradition takes place after we've come home. We have "slides night," as my son calls it. Instead of taking photos as prints, I take several rolls of slides. One night we all pile into the family room with bowls of popcorn and watch the new slides on the wall over the couch. Then one of us picks a carousel of slides from a past trip to view as well.

All of our traditions evolved pretty naturally. The best ones are made by our children, who love the idea of special days. If you find your family enjoying an event or celebration, ask, "Should we make this a family tradition?" This formalizes the event so that family members can anticipate and appreciate it more.

As you create your own traditions, you reinforce your family's goals and values and build long-term unity and strength.

◈I TIPS FROM THE TRENCHES I◈

◈ When our regular baby-sitter asked if she could bring a friend while she watched our children, we were a little concerned that she would be distracted. But we're glad we said yes. It turned out that our kids enjoyed the two teenagers, who were each able to play with one child. Now, even though we pay a little more, we encourage two baby-sitters at a time.

—Mona, Boston, Massachusetts

◈ The kids used to fight over who got to ride in the front seat until we got a car with air bags on the passenger side. Now they both have to ride in the back for safety reasons. No more arguing!

—Aphie, Harbor Beach, Florida

◈ Take your toddlers to ethnic restaurants—they're often less expensive, kids are introduced to different cultures, the atmosphere can be more casual, and the food (cheese burritos, sweet and sour soup, Indian biryani dishes) are real kid pleasers.

—Ellen, New York City

Epilogue

1997: Sesame Place, a children's theme park in Langhorne, Pennsylvania

My husband and I sit on a shaded bench near Rubber Duckie Pond—in our damp bathing suits and rubber flip-flops, locker keys around our wrists, soggy beach towels at our side—while we watch our six- and eight-year-old go down yet another water slide. It is the end of a long day for us, and our kids are trying to get the most out of the last hour.

"One more time, Mom!" they shriek, and bound up the steps, headed for Runaway Rapids.

We smile wanly and return to people watching. It occurs to me that my husband and I have somehow managed to survive the first few years of rearing two children with just a few scars. As babies, then toddlers, then preschoolers, Annie and Alex plowed through the measles, the mumps, one broken arm, three double strollers, two cases of conjunctivitis, several day care centers and four teenage baby-sitters. My husband and I experienced a multitude of sleepless nights, many minor skirmishes, one or two major battles, two nights apart from the kids for our tenth wedding anniversary, and four annual weekends here at Sesame Place. Although at times those years seemed to trudge by in slow motion, it suddenly hits me that time actually flew by in a blink. The next block of years—middle school and high school—seem only minutes away.

Since becoming parents, my husband and I have had to make a radical shift in our vacationing locales. We used to spend our summers touring the Champagne wineries of Rien, Verdi's birthplace in Busseto, the Alhambra in Granada. We did try, in those first few years after the kids were born, to continue that kind of vacation ("By golly, our lifestyle won't have to change!"), but after doing Venice with a stroller and the wine country with toddlers, we gave up. That's how the four of us end up each year standing in line at 8:45 in the morning at the gates of this water theme park.

We are old hands here, so we know our way around—unlike most of the other parents who have a look of mild panic on their faces as they stare at the hordes of preschoolers and strollers at Little Bird's Birdbath and Ernie's Waterworks. We know, for example, to get here early, rent a locker first, hit the newest water rides before the lines start, and save the Bird Show for after lunch.

There is a cross section of parents here—yuppie parents, weight-lifting parents, inner-city parents, suburban parents, hippie parents—all looking their absolute worst. As all parents of two children know, it is impossible to look good and be with your kids at the same time. My husband and I are part of this specialized crowd—our bodies battered by childbirth and age—and we are, like the others here, determined to be good parents, at least for this day.

Mothers in conservative one-piece bathing suits—damp, frizzy hair and no mascara—lunge over strollers or, holding infants, ease themselves into inner tubes. Fathers—bald spots exposed, stomachs protruding, glasses spattered with water—carry four-year-olds on their shoulders. Here at Sesame Place, there are no babes. For a moment earlier in the day I thought I saw one—a babe, that is, and a male babe at that. Sort of a Sam Sheppard type—looking cool in his Ray-Bans and jeans, his hand resting on his young son's shoulder. But then he ducked into the locker room. When he reappeared in his bathing suit, squinting into the sunlight, I watched him slip on the dreaded water socks and strap on his neon pink fanny pack. Out came a pacifier, which he used to flag down his wife, who was pushing a stroller. Good-bye Babe, hello Dad.

There is a small commotion behind us, and we see Cookie Monster and Elmo strolling down the street, followed by squeals from kids, who circle them and take turns posing while their parents take photos. Our kids, however, barely turn around as they head for Sky Splash. There was a time when they, too, would squeal in delight, but that was last year. This year, I fear, they're getting older—too old for this place. We have already heard rumblings in the backseat on the way here about Six Flags Great Adventure and other water parks with scarier rides. My husband adamantly disagrees, suggesting another visit here next summer. In his mind, as long as we keep coming to Sesame Place, our children will never have to grow up. But I think in his heart he realizes this is our last trip here.

The stress level has risen at the park—surely the best way to gauge the end of the day. Tensions are higher, parents are less patient and cheerful, children have developed the Whine. Small family fights are developing around us.

"Where *were* you?" a woman screams at her husband. "It takes forty-five minutes to buy film?"

"I thought we were meeting at that birdbath place . . ." His voice trails off.

It is almost time to go. Soon we will take our tired but happy children back to our nearby chain motel. In the morning, our complimentary continental breakfast will include Sugar Smacks, Hawaiian Punch, and coffee with nondairy creamer on a Styrofoam tray. We will dine in the lobby while CNN blares from a wall-mounted television. The children rave over this breakfast event. The adults try not to compare it to hot croissants, café au lait, and cloth napkins on a bougainvillea-covered balcony in Aix-en-Provence.

"Kids! How about a last rice down Big Bird's Rambling River?" my husband asks hopefully. By tradition, this is our final family event of the day. My husband and I enjoy this inner-tube ride— we can wear our sunglasses and have a conversation while magic technology gently moves us down the "river" and around the park. Although this morning our kids had rejected the river as too boring, now—as if they know this piece of their childhood is over, that next year we will all move on to bigger parks and more sophisticated vacations—they smile sweetly at us. It is as if they are the parents and we are the children. They agree to this last ride.

And so, as the sun drops behind Snuffy's Snack Bar the four of us line up at the concrete steps of Rambling River. At the lifeguard's nod, we squat in unison into our inner tubes, join hands, and float away together, one last time.

Recommended Reading

PREGNANCY, BIRTH, BREAST-FEEDING

England, Pam, and Rob Horowitz, *Birthing from Within: An Extra-Ordinary Guide to Childbirth* (Albuquerque, N.M.: Partera Press, 1998).

Kaufmann, Elizabeth, *Vaginal Birth After Cesarean* (Alameda, Calif.: Hunter House, 1996).

Tamony, Katie, *Your Second Pregnancy: What to Expect This Time* (Chicago: Chicago Review Press, 1995).

Torgus, Judy, and Gwen Gotsch, *The Womanly Art of Breastfeeding* (New York: Plume, 1997).

FOR PARENTS

Bray, James, and John Kelly, *Stepfamilies: Love, Marriage and Parenting the First Decade* (New York: Broadway Books, 1998).

Brazelton, T. Berry, M.D., *Working and Caring* (Reading, Mass.: Addison Wesley Publishing, 1987).

Editors of *Parents* magazine, *The Parents Answer Book: From Birth Through Age Five* (New York: Golden Books, 1998).

Ellis, Elizabeth, *Raising a Responsible Child* (New York: Birch Lane Press, 1996).

Evans, John, *Marathon Dad: Setting a Pace That Works for Working Fathers* (New York: Avon, 1998).

Eyre, Richard and Linda, *Three Steps to a Strong Family* (New York: Fireside, 1994).

Faber, Adele, and Elaine Mazlish, *Siblings Without Rivalry* (New York: Avon Books, 1987).

Gray, John, *Children Are from Heaven* (New York: HarperCollins, 1999).

Herman, Deborah, *The Complete Idiot's Guide to Motherhood* (New York: Alpha Books 1999).

Hochschild, Arlie, *The Second Shift* (New York: Avon, 1997).

Lansky, Vicki, *Welcoming Your Second Baby* (Minnetonka, Minn.: Book Peddlers, 1995).

Leman, Kevin, *The Birth Order Book* (Ada, Mich.: Spire Books, 1985).

Leonard, Joan, *Tales from Toddler Hell: My Life As a Mom* (New York: Pharos Books, 1991).

Maushart, Susan, *The Mask of Motherhood* (New York: The New Press, 1999).

Nelson, Jane, *Positive Discipline for Preschoolers* (Rocklin, Calif.: Prima Publishing, 1995).

Samalin, Nancy, *Loving Each One Best* (New York: Bantam Books, 1996).

FOR CHILDREN

Alexander, Martha, *When the New Baby Comes, I'm Moving Out* (New York: Dial Press, 1979).

Berenstain, Jan and Stan, *The Berenstain Bears' New Baby* (New York: Random House, 1974).

Chambliss, Maxie, *I'm a Big Brother* (also *I'm a Big Sister*) (New York: Morrow Junior Books, 1997).

Cole, Babette, *Mommy Laid an Egg* (San Francisco: Chronicle Books, 1993).

Cole, Joanna, *The New Baby at Your House* (New York: Morrow Junior Books, 1998).

Corey, Dorothy, *Will There Be a Lap for Me?* (Morton Grove, Ill.: Albert Whitman and Co., 1992).

Fearnley, Jan, *A Special Something* (New York: Hyperion for Children, 2000).

Hines, Anna Grossnickle, *Big Like Me* (New York: Greenwillow, 1989).

Lansky, Vicki, *A New Baby at KoKo Bear's House* (Minnetonka, Minn.: Book Peddlers, 1987).

Palatini, Margie, *Good As Goldie* (New York: Hyperion for Children, 2000).

Ziefert, Harriet, *Waiting for Baby* (New York: Holt, 1998).

About the Author

JOAN LEONARD is a former contributing editor of *Parents* magazine and the author of *What to Do to Improve Your Child's Manners* and *Tales from Toddler Hell*. Her articles have appeared in numerous magazines and newspapers including *Good Housekeeping, Woman's Day, Glamour, Ladies Home Journal, Redbook, Parenting, Child*, and *The New York Times*. She lives in Northport, New York, with her husband and two children.